Happy Wedding, Unhappy Marriage

An Honest Look at Why Marriages Fall Apart Today

Dedication

To every couple that tried,
To every partner that stayed too long,
And to those brave enough to walk away…
this book is for you.

And to my wife,
who has stood beside me not just as a companion,
but as a true teammate through every season of our marriage…
thank you for being my anchor, my ally,
and for reminding me that partnership is built, not found.

This book holds truths that many fear to speak.
But we lived through them, not against each other,
but with each other.

For us.
For love.
For understanding what forever really takes.

Table of Contents

Bonus Section: Reconnect or Reflect

For Therapists & Counsellors: Tools for Session Work

Preface

They're educated. Independent. Well-traveled. They fell in love or chose wisely in an arranged setup. They had Instagrammable weddings, supportive parents, and dream honeymoons. And now… they're in therapy. Or quietly miserable. Or speaking to lawyers.

What's going on?

This book is born from a question that echoes across dinner tables, therapy rooms, legal offices, and sleepless nights:
Why are so many modern marriages falling apart?

We live in an age of unmatched freedom and opportunity. And yet, relationships, especially the one institution we're taught to build our lives around are more fragile than ever. Divorce rates are climbing. Emotional intimacy is dropping. Infidelity is easier. Expectations are higher. And the tools to deal with all of it? Often missing.

This isn't a book that blames men. Or women. Or culture. Or modernity.
It's not about nostalgia for the past, nor a glorification of "how things used to be."

It is, however, an honest attempt to shine a light on:

• Why marrying later in life often makes adjustment harder

- How dating apps and casual sex are reshaping commitment
- The impact of financial stress, school fees, and cost of living
- The trauma of parental interference and unsolicited advice
- What happens when people marry for status, not love
- The invisible suffering of LGBTQ+ individuals forced into heterosexual marriages
- How children become both a source of joy and pressure
- And why many couples feel lonelier together than they did alone

We'll also talk about mental health, gender roles, emotional labor, the myth of "forever," and the new age of conscious partnerships. This book will not pretend there is one solution. Instead, it will offer you something more valuable: clarity.

Whether you're single and unsure, married and struggling, divorced and healing, or simply curious, this book is for you. It doesn't judge. It doesn't prescribe. But it will ask hard questions. And it may answer some you've been too afraid to voice.

Because love isn't dead. It's just asking us to evolve.

Welcome to the unfiltered truth about modern marriage.

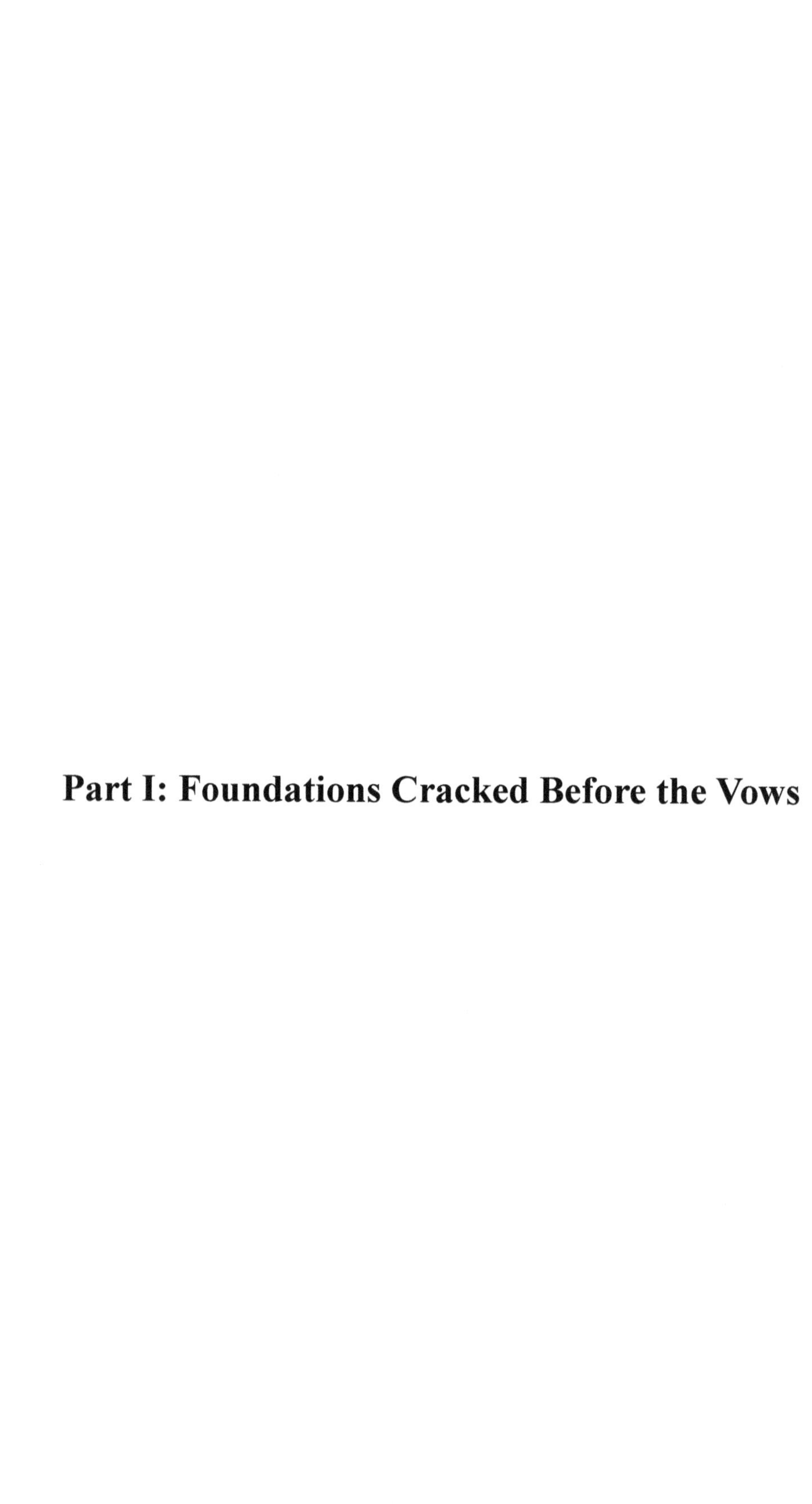

Part I: Foundations Cracked Before the Vows

Chapter 1: The Myth of Forever

They told us that love is enough.
That once you find "the one," everything else falls into place.
That you'll marry, settle down, and somehow, magically forever will just happen.

We believed them.

But in homes around the world today, across India, across cultures, across generations, forever is breaking down. Couples who had dream weddings, years of dating, mutual respect, and even love… are now sleeping back-to-back, scrolling on their phones in silence. Or fighting in therapy. Or quietly pretending for the sake of children, parents, and society. Or walking out.

So what went wrong?

This chapter isn't here to dismiss love. It's here to question how we've defined it and why that definition is proving dangerous.

The Disneyfication of Love

We grew up watching people fall in love in two hours, then roll the credits. No fights about finances. No in-laws. No trauma. No sexless nights. No bills. No broken communication.

Movies, books, TV shows, even Instagram influencers today, paint love as the destination. "Once you find the right person," they imply, "life becomes easy."

That's a lie.
Love is not the finish line. It's the starting gun.

The Modern Pressure to Be Perfect

Today's couples are under more pressure than ever before.

You're expected to:

- Be emotionally available
- Physically attractive
- Financially stable
- Sexually compatible
- Spiritually aligned
- Socially aware
- Great with kids
- Great with each other's families
- And still have date nights

All while navigating rising costs, two-career households, burnout, and parenting. Our grandparents' marriages weren't necessarily happier, they were just simpler. There were fewer choices, clearer gender roles, lower expectations, and more tolerance. Today, we

want equality, freedom, and emotional fulfilment and that's good.
But we've not been taught how to build that.

So when forever starts feeling like a trap instead of a dream,
couples panic. "Maybe I married the wrong person," they think.
Often, that's not true.
What's true is: you were sold the wrong definition of marriage.

Romance Isn't Partnership

Falling in love is easy. Living together in alignment takes grit.
Romance is soft. Marriage is structure.
Romance is emotion. Marriage is responsibility.
Romance says, "I'll love you no matter what."
Marriage whispers, "Will you still love me after I haven't slept,
haven't healed, and don't have answers?"

We treat weddings like the peak of a mountain. In reality, they're
basecamp. The climb begins after the honeymoon. That's when
patterns surface. Unhealed trauma appears. The emotional labor
begins. The financial pressure hits. The daily grind begins. And
no one teaches us how to climb together.

The Decline of "Adjusting"

In older generations, people married younger, before they were
fully formed. They grew together. Learned to adjust. Made
sacrifices before individual egos were cemented.

Now, people marry in their 30s. They come into marriage with:

- Firm routines
- Personal boundaries
- Career identities
- Past relationships
- Financial independence
- High standards

While this maturity can be an asset, it also means we're less flexible. We're used to living life a certain way. We've built lives around ourselves. And it's very hard to suddenly merge that with someone else's entire world.

The Wedding Was Great. The Marriage Isn't.

Weddings today are spectacles. Carefully curated. Filtered. Documented. Posted. But what happens when the likes fade, the reels stop, and it's just two humans, trying to co-exist?

No one teaches us what to do after the wedding.
How to disagree with love.
How to fight fair.
How to reconnect when you feel distant.
How to deal with rejection.
How to forgive.
How to grieve.
How to stay.

And so, we end up chasing a fantasy, of forever that feels effortless.
When effort comes, we assume it's a sign of failure.
It isn't.
Effort is the price of anything meaningful. Including marriage.

Redefining Forever

Forever isn't guaranteed. It's not magical. It's not promised. It's built, brick by brick, conversation by conversation, mistake by mistake, and repair by repair.

If we want modern marriages to survive, we have to stop asking:

"Did I marry the right person?"

And start asking:

"Are we both willing to become the right people, for each other, again and again?"

Because happy weddings don't guarantee happy marriages.
Only realistic expectations and emotional growth do.

Chapter 2: Set in Our Ways – The Late Marriage Dilemma

It sounds ideal:
"You should get married only when you're ready."
And in theory, it is.

Marrying later often means:

- Financial independence
- More life experience
- Better emotional awareness
- Clearer deal-breakers
- Higher standards

But it also brings something few people talk about emotional rigidity.

By the time most urban couples marry today, especially in their late 20s or 30s, they're already living individually designed lives. They've developed their own:

- Sleep patterns
- Morning routines
- Food preferences
- Career priorities
- Boundaries
- Social circles
- Coping mechanisms

They've often lived alone, dated multiple people, traveled solo, perhaps even lived abroad.
They've become whole individuals, but not team players.

When Two Fully Formed People Collide

Earlier generations married at 20 or 21. They grew up together. They made decisions together. They compromised without even calling it that, because they were still figuring themselves out.

Today, people marry at 30+, with a decade or more of personalisation behind them.

Now, that's not bad. But here's the twist:
The more we know what we want, the harder it becomes to live with someone who wants something different.

And marriage?
It's a daily lesson in compromise.

The Danger of "Non-Negotiable's"

You'll hear it often from modern couples:
"I have my own way of doing things."
"This is how I've always been."
"I need my space."
"I can't deal with that."

These are valid boundaries, but too many boundaries harden into walls.

Marriage isn't about dissolving your identity.
But it does require flexibility.
If everything is non-negotiable, what's the point of being in a partnership?

You're not roommates with benefits. You're co-creating a life.
And if neither of you is willing to bend even slightly, the marriage breaks instead.

Independence or Isolation?

The modern value system glorifies independence:
"Be whole before you get married."
"Never depend on anyone."
"Don't lose yourself."

All good advice, until taken to the extreme.

When two ultra-independent people get married, they often end up:
- Avoiding conflict by avoiding each other
- Solving problems alone
- Sharing space but not emotions
- Prioritising freedom over connection

Over time, they become emotionally isolated, even while sleeping in the same bed.

The marriage becomes a logistics agreement, not a bond.

The Illusion of Compatibility

We assume that marrying later means we'll choose "better." That we're more emotionally mature. That we'll avoid the mistakes our parents made.

But often, what we end up doing is over-filtering.

We treat marriage like an app setting:

- Must earn this much
- Must believe in X
- Must never do Y
- Must eat this
- Must not do that

Instead of building compatibility through shared experiences and empathy, we try to engineer it like a checklist.

And when our partner inevitably disappoints one of those filters? We start questioning everything.

Past Luggage, Present Problems

Late marriages often mean more emotional baggage:

- More exes
- More heartbreak
- More trust issues
- More skepticism
- More "I've seen enough of the world to know what I don't want."

But what about learning how to heal?
What about learning how to rebuild trust with a new person?

Too many people carry past damage into a present relationship and expect their partner to clean it up.
Without even realising it, we let old wounds dictate new dynamics.

The Biological Clock Paradox

In heterosexual marriages, especially in India, marrying later also triggers another kind of pressure:
The urgency to have children quickly.

This often rushes couples through:

- Setting up a home
- Building communication
- Enjoying early married life
- Establishing emotional intimacy

Instead, they're thrown immediately into:

- Fertility stress
- Family pressure
- Parenting fatigue
- Sleepless nights

The marriage doesn't get time to breathe. It just begins under pressure and stays there.

So, Should We Marry Early Again?

No.
This isn't about going back to child marriages or regressive expectations.
It's about recognising that every age comes with trade-offs.

Marrying late brings emotional depth.
Marrying early allows shared growth.
Both require awareness, effort, and adaptability.

The key isn't the age.
It's the attitude.

Adjusting Is Not Weakness

In today's world, adjusting has become a bad word.
People mistake compromise for oppression.
But in truth, every lasting marriage is built on some level of adjustment.

Adjustment doesn't mean losing yourself.
It means making space for another person's world, needs, pain, and love.
It means knowing when to bend and when to hold your ground.
It means learning, not just to love, but to live with love.

Because love isn't enough.
You also need humility, patience, and the willingness to stretch.

Forever doesn't break because people marry late.
It breaks because they enter with closed minds and open suitcases, ready to pack up and leave at the first sign of discomfort.

Chapter 3: Burned Out Before the Vows

We wanted freedom. We got options.
We wanted choice. We got apps.
We wanted love. We got burned, again and again, until we didn't know what love even looked like anymore.

Before many modern marriages even begin, couples are already emotionally drained. Not from each other, but from everything that came before.

You'd think more experience leads to wiser choices. But what if it's also leading to emotional exhaustion?
We're not walking into marriage hopeful. We're walking in guarded.

The Ghosts in the Room

Every marriage now includes at least two invisible guests:

- The people we dated before
- The people we couldn't forget

Breakups may end on paper, but they linger in memory:

- "My ex used to appreciate me more."
- "She never reacted like this."
- "He never made me feel so small."
- "I hope this doesn't become like my last relationship."

We compare without realising.
We guard ourselves unnecessarily.
We hold back out of fear.
And without knowing it, we start expecting the new person to make up for old pain.

That's not love.
That's emotional outsourcing.

Dating App Fatigue

Swipe. Match. Ghost. Repeat.
Welcome to the modern dating cycle.

Dating apps promised connection. Instead, they delivered:

- Superficial attraction
- Endless choice
- Shallow attention spans
- No patience for effort
- Constant FOMO

We now approach people like products:

- "Not tall enough."
- "Not ambitious enough."
- "She sounds clingy."
- "He replies too fast : desperate."

- "She's probably talking to five others."

Apps gave us convenience, but robbed us of curiosity.
They made us think we deserve perfection, without the discomfort of discovery.

So by the time we actually find someone worth keeping, many of us have already developed the muscle of detachment.

We're trained to exit, not trained to stay.

Overthinking Kills Intimacy

Modern love is hyper-analytical.
We Google red flags.
We quiz our partners.
We run emotional background checks.
We monitor "attachment styles."
We watch TikToks on "narcissists vs. empaths."
We make therapy terms part of daily conversation and sometimes use them as weapons.

It's good to be aware. But awareness without trust turns into paranoia.

Intimacy requires letting someone in.
But most of us are now in protect mode, not connect mode.

So we pre-filter, over-analyse, test, and doubt.

Then wonder why the spark died early.
Truth is, it never had space to catch fire.

Baggage, Not Luggage

Let's get one thing straight:
Everyone has baggage.

That's not the problem.

The problem is:

- When we refuse to acknowledge it
- When we expect our partner to carry it
- When we dump it in the middle of the relationship without care

You don't need to be healed to be in a marriage.
But you need to be responsible for your healing.

A good marriage is not a rehab centre.
It's a partnership between two adults who are aware of their wounds and don't weaponise them.

The Mask of "I'm Fine"

Many of us have learned to fake confidence. We say:

- "I'm independent."

- "I don't need anyone."
- "I'm not emotional."
- "I've moved on."
- "I've worked on myself."

But underneath, there's often fear, shame, abandonment, anxiety, or low self-worth.
We perform strength. We hide hurt. And then when marriage demands emotional vulnerability, we panic.

We don't know how to:

- Be seen
- Be raw
- Be honest without being ashamed
- Ask for comfort without sounding needy

So we withdraw. Or lash out. Or shut down.

And our partner thinks we're cold.
When really, we're just… tired.

Premature Emotional Burnout

By the time many people get married, they're already exhausted from dating, heartbreak, rejections, and self-reinvention.

They come in with low trust, low patience, and high caution.

They want the benefits of marriage, without the emotional exposure.

But the truth is:
Marriage is emotionally expensive.
It asks for openness. For presence. For hard conversations. For giving your heart again, even when it was broken before.

And if you're too burned out to try, it doesn't matter how good the other person is.

The Real Questions We Should Be Asking

Before getting married, people often ask:

- "Do I love them?"
- "Are we compatible?"
- "Will they make me happy?"

But maybe we also need to ask:

- "Am I still angry at someone from my past?"
- "Have I truly processed my last breakup?"
- "Am I emotionally present or just filling a gap?"
- "Am I looking for healing or hiding?"

Because when we marry to escape loneliness, to prove something, or to erase someone, we're not building love.
We're building distraction.

And distraction never lasts.

Heal, Then Connect

This isn't a call for perfection.
It's a call for honest readiness.

Yes, we're all wounded.
Yes, we're all carrying stories.
Yes, we all have fears.

But healing means you're aware of your patterns, and willing to take ownership for how they affect others.

That's the real work.

Because if we keep marrying while emotionally burnt out, guarded, cynical, or afraid…
We'll keep having happy weddings and unhappy marriages.

Chapter 4: Apps, Affairs & One-Night Stands

Monogamy was once enforced by culture.
Now, it's a choice.

The digital world has given us incredible freedom, but also endless access.
Temptation isn't lurking in a smoky bar anymore.
It's in your pocket.
On your lunch break.
While your partner sleeps beside you.

One swipe. One message. One emoji.
And you're no longer fully present in your marriage.

Modern relationships are not just competing with other people, they're competing with constant novelty, instant validation, and the illusion of better options.

Hookup Culture and the "Backup Plan" Mentality

Dating apps were designed to help people find love.
But they've evolved into catalogues of desire.

Apps like Tinder, Bumble, Hinge, Grindr, and even Instagram DMs have normalised:

- Casual hookups
- Emotional flirting outside relationships
- Short-term validation over long-term investment
- Keeping options open "just in case"

Even married people are swiping, sometimes for thrills, sometimes for attention, sometimes for more.

This is no longer rare.
It's quiet. Hidden. Often not even physical.
But deeply damaging.

It sends a message to your subconscious and your spouse:

"You are not enough.
I'm still looking."

Affairs in the Age of Access

Infidelity today doesn't require effort.
You don't need a hotel room or a second phone.
You just need Wi-Fi and a little secrecy.

And here's the truth:
Affairs don't always start in the bedroom.
They start in conversation.
In late-night replies.
In DMs that feel "harmless."
In emotional intimacy that slowly shifts outside the marriage.

By the time it turns physical, the emotional boundary has already been crossed.

And whether it's physical or digital, the impact is real:

- Trust breaks
- Self-esteem shatters
- Intimacy fades
- Resentment builds

An affair is not just a betrayal of your partner, it's a betrayal of the shared container your marriage was meant to be.

The "Grass is Greener" Delusion

The swipe culture trains us to think:

- "There's always someone better."
- "I shouldn't settle."
- "If this person annoys me, I'll find another."

We've started applying consumer logic to commitment.

We forget that every person will:

- Have flaws
- Annoy us
- Disappoint us
- Require work

But we're not trained for repair anymore. We're trained for replacement.

Unfortunately, marriage doesn't work like Amazon Prime. You can't return your partner and order a new one before the weekend.

One-Night Stands: The New Normal?

Casual sex is now often framed as empowerment. And in some contexts, it can be.
But when one-night stands become habitual coping mechanisms for:

- Loneliness
- Boredom
- Validation
- Rebellion
- Anger toward a spouse

…it's no longer freedom. It's escapism.

We've mistaken momentary pleasure for meaningful connection.
We've started outsourcing intimacy.
We're numbing rather than nurturing.

And when this becomes part of married life, openly or secretly, it begins eroding trust at a molecular level.

Emotional Cheating: The Affair No One Talks About

What hurts more than sex?

Emotional intimacy with someone who isn't your spouse.

That one colleague you confide in.
That "friend" who knows more about your marriage than your partner does.
That ex you still talk to every now and then "just to check in."
The person you joke with, vent to, text at midnight, and call when things go wrong.

If your partner knew, would they feel comfortable?
Or would they feel replaced?

If you're giving someone else the best of your attention, energy, and emotional availability, you're already stepping out.

And it's not harmless.
It slowly, silently kills marriages from the inside.

Can Marriages Survive Temptation?

Yes.
But not without:

- Boundaries

- Honesty
- Regular emotional check-ins
- Shared intimacy (not just sexual, but conversational)
- A strong reason to stay in rather than look out

If your partner no longer feels like your favourite person, your safest space, or your first call… start there.

Because the problem isn't the internet.
It's the distance between two people that allowed it to enter in the first place.

Before You Cross the Line…

Ask yourself:

- What am I not getting in my marriage?
- Have I asked for it directly or only hinted?
- Am I reacting to a partner's neglect, or escaping my own fear of intimacy?
- Do I want this person or do I just want to feel wanted?

Because most affairs, DMs, and hookups don't happen because something's missing.
They happen because something's unspoken.

And that silence is what breaks marriages, not the sex.

Rebuild, Don't Replace

Every marriage goes through boredom. Distance. Dry spells.
Doubt.
You will feel attracted to others at some point.
That's human.
What matters is what you do next.

If you use that desire as a cue to explore outside, the marriage
fractures.
If you use that desire as a sign to reconnect inside, the marriage
deepens.

But first, you must recognise that the modern world is built to
distract, not bond.

And only the conscious will stay married now.

Chapter 5: When Love Becomes a Lie

There's a kind of heartbreak that doesn't make it to Instagram.
No dramatic fights. No cheating scandals. No cold war between spouses.
Just one simple truth that makes everything feel like a prison:

"I was never supposed to be in this marriage."

Not because they didn't want love.
But because they were never attracted to the opposite sex in the first place.

The Lie That Begins at the Mandap

In many families, especially in conservative cultures like India, LGBTQ+ people are often raised with two choices:

- Stay closeted and follow the script
- Come out and risk rejection, shame, violence, or being disowned

So they do what's safest:
They perform.

They smile.
They wear the wedding clothes.
They say "I do."
And they pretend.

Sometimes for weeks. Sometimes for years.
Sometimes forever.

But inside, they're breaking.
Because they are sharing a life, a bed, a future, with someone they can never truly love the way that person deserves.

A Marriage with No Consent

Consent isn't just about sex.
It's about truth. About freedom of choice.

And when someone is pressured, manipulated, or emotionally blackmailed into marrying a gender they're not attracted to, even if they nod yes at the wedding… that consent isn't truly given. It's extracted.

This creates a house of cards:

- The straight spouse feels unloved, confused, inadequate
- The closeted spouse feels trapped, guilty, and terrified of being exposed
- Intimacy becomes awkward, avoided, or even traumatic
- Emotional connection suffers
- Children (if any) grow up in confusing silence

And no one is truly happy.

The Spouse Who Never Knew

One of the most devastating roles in these marriages is played by the unaware straight spouse, often a woman.

She gets married, thinking it's a real relationship.
But over time, she notices:

- Avoidance of physical intimacy
- A strange emotional detachment
- Mood swings, secrecy, or depression
- A sense of being unwanted, even when she's done nothing wrong

She may question herself:

"Am I not attractive?"
"Is he seeing someone else?"
"Why does he never touch me?"

What she doesn't realise is… he may be struggling with his own sexuality.
He may never have wanted to marry a woman at all.

And if she finds out?
The pain is double:

- The betrayal of trust

- And the realisation that the entire marriage was based on someone else's fear

This also happens in reverse, with closeted lesbians marrying men.
The outcome is the same: emotional starvation and mutual damage.

The Cost of Silence

Many LGBTQ+ people marry because they think:

- "Maybe I'll learn to love them."
- "I'll try to be normal."
- "At least my parents will be happy."

But repression doesn't lead to peace.
It leads to:

- Depression
- Substance abuse
- Internalised hatred
- Suicidal thoughts
- Sexual dysfunction
- Secret affairs (with same-sex partners)
- Emotional burnout

And often, by the time they leave the marriage (if they ever do), it's too late.

Families are torn. Children are confused. Lives are scarred.

This is the cost of pretending.
And the price is paid by everyone involved.

Why They Stay

People often ask, "Why do they go through with it?"
The answer: Fear.

- Fear of being cut off financially
- Fear of disappointing parents
- Fear of losing siblings, community, status
- Fear of being labeled "unnatural" or "possessed"
- Fear of being assaulted or "converted"
- Fear of not surviving alone

In cultures where family is everything, this fear is very real.
Coming out isn't just a personal act, it's a social death in many cases.

And so, many choose the pain they know over the freedom they're afraid to claim.

And What About the Law?

In some countries including India, same-sex relationships are legal.
But same-sex marriage is still not.

That legal gap becomes a social loophole.
Families use it to pressure LGBTQ+ people into heterosexual marriages, claiming:

"There's no other option.
Get married. Settle down. We won't talk about this again."

No one questions this abuse of marital sanctity.
Because legally, the wedding looks fine.
Emotionally… it's a slow death.

What Needs to Change

This isn't just about queer rights.
It's about human dignity.
It's about informed consent in marriage.
It's about the right to not ruin another person's life because of your own silence.

For society to change:

- LGBTQ+ people must be given safe space to come out
- Families must be educated about what real love and support look like
- Laws must recognise and protect queer marriages, so people don't feel forced into fake ones
- And most importantly, young people must be taught:
- You do not have to marry someone just to make others comfortable

If You're in This Situation

If you're LGBTQ+ and in a heterosexual marriage (or being pressured into one), know this:

- You are not alone.
- You are not broken.
- You are not doing anyone a favour by sacrificing your truth.

And if you're the unsuspecting spouse, know this:

- Their silence isn't always malicious.
- But you deserve clarity. You deserve truth.
- And you are not unlovable, just caught in the wrong story.

Because Marriage Should Be Real

Every marriage is built on some kind of promise.
In LGBTQ+ forced marriages, that promise was never real to begin with.
And no matter how long you try to fake it, love cannot grow where truth is absent.

If we want fewer unhappy marriages, we must stop pushing people into roles they were never meant to play.

Because a wedding isn't worth it, if it costs two people their lives.

Chapter 6: The Ripple Effect of Infidelity

Affairs are rarely just about sex.
They're about escape, validation, resentment, neglect, curiosity, or pain.
Sometimes, they're about power. Sometimes, about loneliness.

But what they're never about is just two people.

An affair is like a stone thrown into a still pond.
The impact may start in one spot, but the ripples travel far, reaching children, extended family, friends, and even generations to come.

And the damage doesn't always look like chaos.
Sometimes, it looks like silence.
Distance.
Disbelief.
And a home that continues to function… but without a soul.

Affairs Don't Just Break Vows. They Break Worlds.

When someone cheats, it doesn't just shake trust, it shakes identity.

The betrayed spouse often asks:

- "Was any of it ever real?"

- "Am I not enough?"
- "How could you do this to us?"
- "Who else knew?"
- "What does this mean for my future?"

They grieve not just the relationship, but the story they thought they were living.

Meanwhile, the person who cheated may spiral into:

- Guilt
- Denial
- Anger at being caught
- Shame so deep they start self-sabotaging
- Emotional numbness
- A desperate need to justify their actions

And if the affair involved someone close, like a family friend, coworker, or neighbour, it adds another layer: betrayal of the entire social circle.

Why People Cheat (Even in "Good" Marriages)

Contrary to popular belief, many affairs happen in marriages that seem fine on the outside.

Common triggers:

- Feeling emotionally ignored
- Lack of appreciation
- Boredom or stagnancy
- Sexual frustration or incompatibility
- A desire to feel desired again
- A craving for novelty or adventure
- A subconscious act of revenge

Sometimes, the affair isn't about the other person at all.
It's about how the cheater feels when they're with that person:
Seen. Wanted. Alive.

But the truth is, if you're willing to destroy a life for a feeling,
you're not ready for marriage.

The Children Always Feel It

Even if they don't know the details, kids always sense the shift:

- The tension
- The avoidance
- The anger
- The crying behind locked doors
- The sudden distance between parents

Children internalise more than we realise.

Some blame themselves.
Some become hyper-independent.

Some lose trust in love altogether.
Some grow up repeating the same patterns.

And years later, when they begin their own relationships, they carry the trauma of betrayal they never even committed.

The Fallout Doesn't Stop at the Door

Infidelity affects:

- **Parents**: who feel shame, anger, or helplessness watching their child's marriage collapse
- **Siblings**: who take sides, often breaking family unity
- **Friends**: who awkwardly withdraw or feel pressured to choose loyalty
- **In-laws**: who feel humiliated or enraged
- **Communities**: especially in conservative cultures, where the affair becomes gossip, and the betrayed spouse becomes a subject of pity or blame

It's not just a private mistake.
It becomes a public fracture.

Can Marriages Survive Infidelity?

Yes… but not without massive effort.

Some couples manage to rebuild. But it takes:

- Complete transparency
- Time for grief
- No gaslighting or blame-shifting
- A willingness to understand what led to the affair, not just condemn it
- Therapy, often individual and couples therapy
- The cheater taking full responsibility without being defensive

Most of all, it takes the betrayed partner wanting to stay… not out of shame or obligation, but because they see the potential for something new, not just a return to what was broken.

When Rebuilding Is Worse Than Leaving

Sometimes, staying is more damaging than walking away.

Especially when:

- The cheater refuses to cut off contact with the third person
- There's no real remorse, just damage control
- The betrayal is part of a pattern, not a mistake
- The emotional abuse becomes worse
- Children are growing up in a war zone

Forgiveness doesn't always mean reconciliation.
You can forgive and still choose to walk away.
You can leave and still heal.

Staying is noble… only if it's safe, wanted, and mutual.

What the Affair Revealed

Infidelity often isn't the disease… it's the symptom.
A mirror to the cracks that were already forming:

- The disconnection
- The resentment
- The loss of intimacy
- The unmet needs
- The communication breakdown

That doesn't justify the affair.
But it contextualises it.

Affairs can be a wake-up call.
Or a closing chapter.

Either way, they demand that both partners look at what the
marriage had become… not just what one person did.

Healing After Infidelity (For Both Sides)

If you've been betrayed:

- Feel your grief fully.
- Don't rush forgiveness.
- Seek therapy.

- Stop blaming yourself for someone else's choice.
- Decide what you want, not what society expects.

If you were the one who cheated:

- Own what you did, **without excuses**.
- Be prepared for long-term accountability.
- Understand the pain you've caused, don't minimise it.
- Show up, consistently, without pressure.
- Ask yourself: What was I really escaping from?

Some Things Break for Good Reason

Not all affairs are mistakes.
Some reveal truths we've been hiding:

- That the marriage is over
- That we were mismatched from the start
- That we outgrew each other
- That we never learned how to communicate honestly

In those cases, the affair didn't destroy the marriage.
It just exposed the truth that the marriage was already running on empty.

And sometimes, the most honest act isn't repairing what broke.
It's acknowledging that it's time to stop pretending and start over.

Chapter 7: The Silent Scream

They no longer argue.
They no longer beg to be understood.
They no longer try to prove a point.

At first glance, this silence might look like peace.

But it's not peace.
It's resignation.

It's the kind of silence that grows between two people who once shared everything and now barely share anything at all.

This chapter is about the emotional distance that destroys marriages long before lawyers are ever called.

The Death of Conversation

When a couple stops talking, it's rarely about lack of time.
It's about lack of trust, lack of emotional safety, or the sheer exhaustion of repeating yourself and never being heard.

At first, the silence creeps in slowly:

- One-word answers
- "I'm tired" as a permanent excuse
- Talking about logistics, not feelings
- Avoiding eye contact at dinner

- Going to bed at different times

Eventually, the silence becomes its own language:
A language of detachment.

Why We Stop Speaking

Silence in marriage often follows:

- Repeated fights with no resolution
- Criticism without compassion
- Emotional neglect
- Feeling unheard or dismissed
- Mockery, defensiveness, or stonewalling
- The fear that honesty will lead to conflict or apathy

And once the silence sets in, it becomes easier to maintain than to break.

Why? Because restarting communication feels:

- Vulnerable
- Awkward
- Risky
- Pointless

So both partners retreat into their own corners.
They talk to friends, parents, therapists, or no one at all, except each other.

Loneliness in a Shared Bed

This is one of the deepest forms of pain in marriage:
Being lonely while not alone.

Your partner is physically there, maybe even doing everything "right":
Paying bills, helping with the kids, maintaining the home.

But emotionally?
They feel miles away.

There's no curiosity.
No meaningful eye contact.
No check-ins.
No shared joy.
No comfort during stress.
Just a quiet, dull rhythm of survival.

And sometimes, that hurts more than fighting.

Why Arguments Are Not Always Bad

Fighting can feel ugly, but silence is often more dangerous.

When couples argue, it means:

- They still care
- They still want to be heard

- There's still hope of being understood

But when the fights stop, not because things have improved, but because one or both partners have emotionally checked out, that's when disconnection becomes permanent.

Silence is not always maturity.
Sometimes, it's emotional surrender.

The Passive-Aggressive Marriage

Some silences are not neutral.
They're loaded.

- Withholding affection as punishment
- Giving the silent treatment instead of expressing hurt
- Deliberately ignoring messages or requests
- "Forgetfulness" that's really avoidance
- Sarcastic digs dressed as jokes

This isn't healthy space.
This is emotional warfare in disguise.

It keeps the marriage looking "functional" to outsiders while both people are internally bleeding.

The Loop of Disconnection

Often, silence is cyclical:

One partner feels unheard → starts withdrawing
The other feels neglected → becomes defensive
Communication worsens → resentment builds
Emotional safety erodes → silence deepens

And round it goes.

What began as a small miscommunication becomes a permanent emotional wall.

"We Don't Talk Like We Used To"

It usually starts with one realisation:

"We don't talk anymore. Not really."

You talk about groceries.
About the children.
About bills.
But you no longer talk about dreams.
Or fears.
Or how your day really was.
Or what you're secretly worried about.
Or how you feel unseen, even in a room with them.

This emotional starvation doesn't kill a marriage overnight.
But slowly, it rots the foundation.

Relearning the Lost Art of Talking

You can't rebuild intimacy if you don't talk.
You can't fix what's broken if you can't even name it.

Reconnection starts small:

- A genuine "How are you feeling?"
- Pausing to listen instead of replying
- Asking deeper questions beyond routine
- Creating space without phones or distractions
- Speaking honestly, even if your voice shakes
- Replacing blame with curiosity
- Choosing kindness, even when it's hard

It's not always comfortable.
But it's the only way out of the silent scream.

Warning Signs of a Dead Conversation Pattern

If you find yourselves:

- Always talking through the kids
- Never discussing emotions
- Avoiding each other's company
- Feeling more seen by friends or strangers
- Not remembering the last time you truly connected

Then the silence has become chronic.
And it needs to be addressed, **now**, not later.

Because unchecked silence doesn't stay silent forever.
Eventually, it turns into resentment.
Or indifference.
Or infidelity.
Or departure.

Ask Each Other And Mean It

Here are five questions that can reopen closed hearts:

- "What have you been needing lately but haven't asked for?"
- "Is there something I do that makes you feel unseen?"
- "When was the last time you felt really close to me?"
- "What's something you miss about the early days of us?"
- "How can I show up for you better right now?"

You may be surprised at what still lives beneath the silence.

Silence Can Heal or Destroy

Silence isn't always bad.
Sometimes, it's a sacred pause.

But left unchecked, it becomes a graveyard of unspoken pain.

A marriage can survive stress, fights, dry spells, even betrayal.

But a marriage without emotional communication is like a house without oxygen.

It looks fine…
Until everything collapses.

So if your home is quiet in all the wrong ways… **speak.**
Not because it's easy.
But because silence isn't peace.
It's a warning.

Part II: Inside the Marital Storm

Chapter 8: Sex in the Age of Shame & Screens

Sex used to be private.

Now it's everywhere, yet nowhere where it should be: between couples who love each other, trust each other, and feel safe enough to explore.

We live in a world flooded with sexual content.

But inside many marriages?

Sex has become awkward. Silent. Absent. Or weaponised.

Some couples are having less sex.

Others are having robotic sex.

Some are mismatched in desire.

Some haven't touched each other in months or years.

And what's worse: many aren't even talking about it.

This chapter is about what happens when the most intimate part of your marriage becomes the most avoided.

The Slow Extinction of Desire

No couple plans to stop having sex.

It just… fades.

One person gets tired.

The other feels rejected.

A new baby arrives.

Work takes over.

Hormones shift.

Resentment simmers.

Screens replace attention.

Intimacy turns into routine.

And before they know it, they're roommates with rings.

The Silence Around Sex

Sex is still a taboo conversation, especially in conservative societies.

Even in therapy rooms, couples struggle to say:

- "I feel unwanted."
- "I want more."
- "I don't feel safe."
- "I have needs I'm afraid to share."
- "I feel judged or inadequate."

This silence breeds:

- Mistrust
- Assumptions
- Insecurity
- Emotional distance
- Secret frustration

- And sometimes, infidelity

When sex dies and no one talks about it, the relationship decays silently.

The Shame We Inherit

Many people enter marriage with shame around sex:

- "Good girls don't ask for it."
- "Men always want it, women tolerate it."
- "Talking about sex is dirty."
- "Desire is dangerous."
- "Exploration is sin."

So when they should be opening up about sex in a committed, loving partnership, they stay silent, awkward, or judgmental.

This shame often comes from:

- Cultural conditioning
- Religious guilt
- Lack of sex education
- Childhood trauma
- Negative past experiences

The result? A bedroom that feels more like a courtroom than a playground.

Mismatched Libidos

One of the most common issues in marriage:
One person wants it more. The other doesn't.

But here's what makes it worse:

- The one with higher desire feels rejected, ashamed, or starved
- The one with lower desire feels pressured, guilty, or defective

And if this isn't talked about openly with empathy, it creates:

- Avoidance
- Manipulation
- Resentment
- Performance without pleasure

Libido mismatches are common.
But silence turns them into suffering.

Screens vs. Skin

Porn. Instagram. Fantasy. Texting. Sexting.
We are overstimulated outside our marriage and emotionally undernourished inside it.

Some people find it easier to turn to:

- Porn (instead of awkward intimacy)
- DMs (instead of direct communication)
- Fantasy (instead of vulnerability)

Why?

Because screens don't judge.
They don't reject.
They don't ask for emotional effort.

But they also don't love you.
They don't hold you.
They don't heal you.

And when they replace your partner, they start to reshape your brain and expectations.

Sexual Compatibility Isn't About Tricks, It's About Safety

Good sex in marriage doesn't require porn-star moves.
It requires:

- Trust
- Curiosity
- Emotional safety
- Openness to learning together
- Willingness to talk about discomfort
- Freedom to explore without fear or shame

Sex is an emotional experience, especially in long-term relationships.
Without safety, desire dies.
Without intimacy, pleasure fades.

When Sex Becomes a Weapon

Sometimes, couples use sex (or the lack of it) to:

- Punish
- Control
- Manipulate
- Withhold love
- Assert dominance
- Shame the other

This turns intimacy into a battleground.

It's no longer about connection, it's about power.
And over time, it becomes toxic.
Some people even tolerate sex they don't want or initiate it out of obligation.

That's not consent. That's compliance.
And it leaves emotional scars.

Can Sex Come Back?

Yes, if both partners are:

- Willing to talk
- Open to help (therapy, books, doctors)
- Honest about needs
- Patient with healing
- Committed to exploring together, not blaming

It might take time.

It might involve discomfort.

But reviving a sexless or struggling sex life is possible when shame is replaced by trust.

5 Questions to Start the Conversation

- "How do you feel about our physical intimacy lately?"
- "Is there something you want that we haven't talked about?"
- "What makes you feel most connected to me?"
- "Are there things that turn you off that I don't realise?"
- "Would you be open to exploring this together without pressure?"

You don't need to have all the answers.

You just need the courage to start asking.

Don't Let the Bedroom Be a Dead End

In happy marriages, the bedroom is not just about sex.

It's about:

- Laughter

- Vulnerability
- Comfort
- Touch
- Reassurance
- Safety

If your bedroom feels cold, it's not too late.

Warm it again, with words.
With honesty.
With patience.
With effort.

Because while love can survive a lot…
It rarely survives being ignored, rejected, or replaced.

Chapter 9: Between the Sheets, But Worlds Apart

You can share a bed and still feel alone.
You can kiss, but feel no warmth.
You can touch, but feel no spark.

Many modern marriages crumble not from the absence of sex, but from the absence of connection around sex.

Because while every other aspect of the relationship is discussed, finances, parenting, responsibilities, sex remains a ghost topic. Unspoken. Avoided. Or worse, faked.

What Does Sexual Incompatibility Really Mean?

It doesn't mean one person is wrong and the other is right.
It means:

- One person might want sex frequently, the other occasionally.
- One may prefer slow intimacy, the other fast passion.
- One might enjoy exploration, the other may find it uncomfortable.
- One sees sex as connection; the other as performance.

And when this gap isn't addressed, the result is not just frustration.

It's rejection, resentment, and detachment.

Sex becomes:

- A duty
- A transaction
- A reward
- Or something to avoid altogether

The Unspoken Hurt of Rejection

Many people feel unloved not because sex is infrequent, but because:

- They feel undesired
- They feel like initiators, not partners
- They are never touched unless it leads to sex
- Their emotional needs are unseen

Others feel trapped because:

- They're tired or touched-out from caregiving
- Sex feels mechanical, rushed, or disconnected
- They've never felt safe enough to express what they want
- Cultural or religious conditioning taught them sex is shameful

The Virginity Obsession: Purity Over Partnership

In some marriages, especially in conservative societies, the issue runs deeper.

Men want a sexually experienced wife, but only if she gains experience with them.
They want:

- A woman who is "adventurous" but "untouched"
- A partner who is "wild in bed" but "traditional at heart"
- A lover who performs, but also submits

And in this bizarre demand, women are:

- Pressured to lie about their past
- Judged for being either "too pure" or "too exposed"
- Shamed if they express desire
- Seen as "used" if they have had previous partners

This toxic virginity fetish does not create trust.
It creates fear, comparison, and constant self-doubt.

It also leads to men being insecure if their partner had more experience, fearing they won't measure up.

But a marriage is not a competition of pasts.
It's a commitment to build something new.

The Porn Generation: Unrealistic Expectations

We live in a hyper-sexualised world where:

- Porn sets impossible standards
- Movies glorify "hot chemistry" over real intimacy
- Social media reduces sexuality to trends and aesthetics

And so:

- Men feel pressure to last longer, perform harder
- Women feel pressure to look perfect, fake pleasure
- Both expect instant arousal without emotional context
- Nobody talks about awkwardness, laughter, slowness, or mistakes

Sex becomes a test, not a conversation.
And when the "performance" fails, ego takes the hit.

"She's Cold." "He's Too Demanding."

These are not always truths.
They are usually surface expressions of deeper wounds.

- Some women have never experienced pleasure and fake it to end it.
- Some men associate sex with their worth and panic when rejected.

- Some partners are recovering from trauma and don't know how to say it.
- Others were never taught that consent, communication, and curiosity matter.

Without space for honesty, shame wins.
And when shame wins, intimacy loses.

Sex Used as a Weapon

In toxic marriages, sex becomes a currency.

- Denied during arguments
- Demanded as a right
- Bartered for vacations, gifts, or silence
- Faked to avoid confrontation
- Forced without care for consent

This isn't intimacy.
It's emotional warfare.

So, What Does Healthy Sexual Communication Look Like?

It's not about:

- "How often"
- "How intense"
- Or "How exciting"

It's about:

- Feeling safe to express your likes and dislikes
- Feeling respected, not judged or mocked
- Feeling wanted, not obligated
- Feeling free, not controlled

Good sex doesn't start in the bedroom.
It starts with trust, gentle curiosity, and emotional presence.

How to Rebuild Intimacy

- **Talk. Ask:** "What makes you feel safe with me sexually?"
- **Be patient**. Don't rush connection. Let it bloom slowly.
- **Name the shame.** Say what's hard to say: "I feel insecure when…"
- **Educate together**. Use books, workshops, or therapy, not porn.
- **Redefine success**. It's not about climax, it's about closeness.
- **Celebrate small wins**. A kiss, a cuddle, a shared fantasy.

Questions Couples Should Ask

- "What do you enjoy that we don't do enough?"
- "What makes you feel disconnected from me sexually?"
- "What are your fears about intimacy?"
- "Have I ever made you feel ashamed about your body or desires?"

- "Do you feel safe saying 'no' or 'not today'?"

The Goal Isn't Perfection, It's Presence

There is no single definition of a "good sex life."
There's only what feels right for both of you.

If you can laugh, pause, explore, cry, try again, and be vulnerable
in each other's arms, you're already winning.

Because sex is not just about bodies.
It's about truth, safety, trust, and surrender.

Chapter 10: Power, Paychecks & Control

They say money can't buy love.
But it can certainly kill it.

In today's marriages, financial compatibility is just as important
as emotional compatibility.
Not because people are materialistic, but because money is power.

And when power is uneven, unclear, or constantly shifting,
marriage becomes a battleground:

- Who earns more?
- Who sacrifices more?
- Who spends more?
- Who gets to decide?

If these questions aren't answered together, they'll be answered
through resentment.

Dual-Income, Double Pressure

Gone are the days when only one person earned.
Now, in most modern marriages, both spouses work.
Sounds great, right?
Financial freedom. Shared responsibility. Equality.

Except…

Many couples discover that two incomes bring two egos, two calendars, two stress cycles, and not enough collaboration.

Instead of sharing the load, they compete over:

- Who's more tired
- Who deserves a break
- Who works harder
- Who's more important

Suddenly, the partnership starts feeling like a scoreboard.

"I Earn More, So I Decide More"

In some marriages, the higher earner begins to assert control, subtly or blatantly:

- Making solo financial decisions
- Dismissing the other's input
- Using money as leverage in arguments
- Expecting gratitude, not discussion

This often leads to emotional imbalance:

- The higher earner feels entitled
- The lower earner feels powerless

The marriage stops being about "us" and starts being about hierarchy.

The Invisible Labor of the Stay-at-Home Spouse

On the flip side, in some households, one spouse stays home (often the woman), while the other earns.

This leads to a different form of tension:

- "What do you even do all day?"
- "I provide. You relax."
- "At least I don't waste time scrolling at home."
- "You wouldn't survive a week at my job."

This ignores a huge truth:
Managing a home, raising children, cooking, planning, and supporting a partner's career is unpaid labor.

Just because it doesn't bring a paycheck doesn't mean it doesn't bring value.

But until couples mutually respect each other's roles, imbalance becomes bitterness.

Financial Secrecy

Many couples think hiding money isn't a big deal.
But secrecy kills trust, even if it's not illegal.

Examples include:

- Secret credit cards
- Hidden purchases
- Unshared debts
- Private investments
- Lending money to family or friends without disclosure

These acts don't just break financial harmony.
They break the emotional contract: We're supposed to be a team.

Financial Abuse: The Silent Control

Financial abuse is rarely discussed, but it's very real.

It includes:

- Controlling all bank accounts
- Giving an "allowance" to the other spouse
- Tracking every rupee
- Forbidding independent spending
- Blocking access to shared funds during fights
- Threatening divorce or abandonment if financial "rules" are broken

This turns the marriage into a dictatorship.
And often, the abused partner stays, not out of love, but financial dependence.

Ego Dressed as Empowerment

Many fights about money aren't really about the money.
They're about:

- Feeling unheard
- Feeling overburdened
- Feeling disrespected
- Feeling less "successful" than the partner
- Fear of becoming irrelevant or replaced

So instead of working together, couples retreat into defensiveness:

- "You don't value what I do."
- "You just want to control me."
- "You don't know how hard I work."
- "You spend like money grows on trees."
- "You only care about your career."

Suddenly, love feels like a negotiation.

Building Financial Intimacy

Money doesn't have to divide you.
It can be a tool to strengthen the bond, if handled with clarity and
mutual respect.

Here's how:

- Set joint financial goals

- Maintain some financial independence, but full transparency
- Discuss spending habits before they become arguments
- Respect differences: one may save, the other may enjoy small luxuries
- Don't punish each other over money
- Talk often, not just during emergencies or blame games
- Acknowledge unpaid labor and emotional labor
- Create joint and individual accounts with agreed boundaries

Most importantly: never use money to control love.

Ask Each Other

- "Do you ever feel financially disrespected or dismissed by me?"
- "What are your biggest fears when it comes to money?"
- "What does financial security mean to you?"
- "Do you think our money reflects our values?"
- "Are we building wealth or building distance?"

If Love Feels Transactional

Sometimes, people stay in marriages not because they're in love, but because they feel financially trapped.
And sometimes, people stay because they're financially benefitting, even if the emotional connection is long gone.

Both are forms of emotional poverty.

If you're using your paycheck as a weapon… you've already lost the relationship.

And if you're silently enduring because you don't have the means to leave… you're not in a marriage.
You're in a contract of quiet survival.

Money doesn't ruin love.
Power does.
The misuse of it. The hoarding of it. The silence around it.

If we want fewer unhappy marriages, we must stop using money as a throne and start using it as a bridge.

Chapter 11: Love for Sale

Not every marriage begins with love.
Some begin with hope.
Some with pressure.
And some begin with a calculation.

"He's rich."
"She looks good on paper."
"He'll take care of me."
"She has connections."
"At least I won't struggle."

Marriage, especially in many parts of the world, is still a social contract first and a relationship second.
But in the modern world, something has shifted.
We're seeing love replaced with leverage.

This chapter is about how money, lifestyle, and legal systems are being used to manipulate marriage, and how both men and women are getting hurt in the process.

Marrying for Money Isn't New. But It's Evolved.

Historically, marriage has always had financial roots:

- Dowries
- Land alliances

- Merging businesses
- Status symbols

But in the 21st century, the strategy has changed:

- Marrying into wealth for lifestyle gains
- Targeting high earners for social mobility
- Choosing partners based on income, not emotional connection
- Entering marriages with exit plans (e.g., high alimony or property leverage)

Is it always intentional? **No.**
Is it happening more often? **Absolutely**.

The Alimony Incentive

In some cases, individuals, especially women, enter marriages with a clear objective:

- Secure a financial safety net
- Quit work entirely
- Build legal leverage
- Exit with a substantial alimony payout

This doesn't mean all women do this.
But when the legal system leans heavily in favour of one gender, it creates loopholes for intentional misuse.

And the men caught in this?

- Often feel used, tricked, and powerless
- Pay not just emotionally, but financially, for years
- Are left fighting to prove innocence or fairness in systems stacked against them

And no one listens.
Because society assumes the man must have been at fault.

When the Law Becomes a Weapon

India's marriage laws and many others around the world, were designed to protect women, especially those without financial independence.

But some individuals now use these laws for revenge, leverage, or gain:

- Filing false domestic violence cases
- Demanding exaggerated alimony
- Accusing in-laws for added pressure
- Blocking divorce proceedings to extract more compensation
- Alienating children to win child custody battles

These tactics not only hurt the accused, but also undermine real victims of abuse and injustice.

We need to ask:

Is the system protecting the vulnerable or enabling manipulation?

Lifestyle Inflation & Hidden Motives

In social-media-fuelled marriages, appearances often matter more than affection.

People chase:

- Lavish weddings
- Influencer-style couples
- Exotic vacations
- "Power couple" branding

And in this chase, many choose partners who can provide that image, even if the relationship itself is hollow.

Some red flags that the marriage may be transactional:

- Zero emotional bonding, even after months
- Interest only in spending, not sharing
- Over-reliance on the spouse's income
- No career ambition or contribution
- Threats of legal action during minor disagreements
- Using children as tools for leverage

At that point, the marriage isn't about love.
It's about leverage.

And What About the Men?

This isn't just about women misusing marriage.
Men do it too:

- Marrying working women to avoid responsibility
- Living off their spouse's income
- Emotionally or financially exploiting ambitious partners
- Threatening legal abandonment when challenged

Marriage misuse has no gender.
It has a mindset: What can I take? instead of What can we build?

Signs You're in a Transactional Marriage

- You feel like an ATM, not a partner
- Love is given only when money flows
- Threats of legal action are frequent
- Your spouse shows zero interest in emotional connection
- Everything becomes a negotiation
- You're more afraid of financial loss than emotional loss

This isn't marriage.
It's legalised manipulation.

Marrying for Stability vs. Marrying for Survival

There's a difference between:

- A woman marrying for support because she lacks options
- And a woman (or man) marrying with the intent to milk the system

We must have compassion for the former, but hold the latter accountable.

No one should be shamed for wanting stability.
But using another person's love, effort, or hard-earned money as a stepping stone or settlement plan is not strategy.
It's abuse.

What Can Be Done?

- Pre-marital agreements (prenups) should become normal, not taboo
- Gender-neutral laws must be introduced for marriage, alimony, and domestic abuse
- Couples must talk openly about money before marriage and revisit regularly
- Financial literacy should be taught before love is legally bound
- Divorce proceedings must evolve to differentiate between genuine need and tactical exploitation

Above all, we must teach people:

If you're not marrying for love, respect, or shared values,
then at least don't pretend that you are.

Ask Yourself (or Each Other)

- "If money didn't matter, would I still choose this person?"
- "Are we building something together or is one person simply benefitting?"
- "Do I trust that this relationship is safe if I lose my income?"
- "Would I still respect this marriage if the lifestyle was taken away?"
- "Do we have financial boundaries that feel fair?"

Marriage Is Not a Marketplace

A real marriage is not a job offer.
Not a sponsorship.
Not a promotion.
Not a transaction.

It's a partnership of effort, sacrifice, emotion, loyalty, mistakes, and growth.

When it becomes a price tag or a payout, it will crumble.

Because no matter how strong the legal contract is, if the heart isn't invested, the marriage will fail.

Chapter 12: The Parenting Avalanche

No one tells you the truth about parenting:
That the moment a child is born, the marriage is reborn too and not always in a better form.

Children bring joy, purpose, laughter, and depth.
But they also bring:

- Sleep deprivation
- Identity crisis
- Financial strain
- Physical exhaustion
- Emotional overload
- And very little time for intimacy

Parenting doesn't destroy a marriage.
It exposes what was already fragile.
It shines a light on imbalance, unspoken resentment, and emotional distance and magnifies it.

This chapter is about how a beautiful child can create a chaotic marriage, not because of who they are, but because of what we're forced to confront once they arrive.

From Romance to Routine

Before kids, couples have time:

- To talk
- To touch
- To connect
- To go on dates
- To be spontaneous
- To be each other's person

After kids, the routine takes over:

- "Did you pack the bag?"
- "Who's doing pickup today?"
- "He didn't nap again."
- "We're out of diapers."
- "Don't wake the baby!"
- "I'm too tired."

And slowly, without realising, you stop seeing your spouse as a lover.

You see them as a co-worker in a very loud, very messy start-up called parenting.

Motherhood Overload, Fatherhood Underplayed

In many homes, especially in patriarchal societies, the mother becomes the default parent, even when both spouses work.

She's expected to:

- Wake up early
- Breastfeed or bottle-feed
- Pack tiffins
- Know the vaccination schedule
- Be emotionally available to the child and the partner
- Look good, stay calm, and somehow still enjoy sex

Meanwhile, the father is often praised for "helping" when he does the bare minimum.

This imbalance:

- Breeds resentment
- Destroys desire
- Makes the woman feel unseen and overworked
- Makes the man feel accused and unappreciated

It's not just about tasks.
It's about the emotional weight of responsibility and who carries it more.

The Child-Centred Marriage

In many modern families, the child becomes the centre of the universe.

Every decision revolves around:

- The child's sleep

- The child's food
- The child's school
- The child's playdates
- The child's mood

Meanwhile, the couple forgets to ask:

- "Are we okay?"
- "When was the last time we held hands, just us?"
- "Do we even remember how to laugh together?"

You don't lose your marriage in one day.
You lose it slowly by putting everything else first.

Shifting Roles, Unspoken Fights

Kids bring out role expectations you didn't know existed:

- "You should've backed me up when I scolded him."
- "Why don't you ever notice when she's sick?"
- "I did bedtime last night. It's your turn."
- "Why am I the one Googling preschools?"
- "Do you even care about how hard this is for me?"

And beneath those lines is a deeper scream:

"I'm tired. I need help. I feel alone."
But if that need isn't acknowledged, it turns into blame, and then bitterness.

The Forgotten Couple

One of the saddest truths of modern marriage is this:
The baby was planned.
The nursery was planned.
The delivery was planned.
But the relationship post-baby was never discussed.

No one said:

- "Let's talk about how our dynamic might change."
- "Let's make a plan to still connect after the baby comes."
- "Let's check in every few weeks, just us."

So what begins as shared joy… becomes silent grief.
A couple still functioning, but no longer feeling.

The Loop of Exhaustion and Avoidance

Here's what often happens:

One partner feels overwhelmed → wants support
The other feels blamed → gets defensive
Both withdraw → intimacy drops
Connection fades → parenting stress grows
More pressure, more silence, more anger
Repeat

Suddenly, even the smallest disagreements become massive fights, because they're not just about parenting.

They're about everything else that's not being said.

Breaking the Cycle

Children deserve a stable, loving home.
But that begins with a stable, loving partnership.

What helps:

- Schedule couple time (yes, schedule it)
- Don't guilt-trip the working partner or the stay-at-home one
- Share mental load, not just physical tasks
- Don't interrupt each other's parenting styles, discuss them offline
- Ask: "How are you doing as a person?" Not just "Did you finish the grocery run?"
- Don't stop flirting
- Don't stop thanking each other
- Be a team, not a task force

Ask Each Other

- "Do you feel like we've lost 'us' since the baby?"
- "What's the hardest part of parenting for you right now?"
- "What do you miss most about how we used to be?"
- "What can I do to make you feel more supported?"
- "When can we plan some time for just the two of us?"

You're Not Failing, You're Just Not Talking

Most parents aren't failing.

They're just too tired to communicate properly.

Too overwhelmed to notice they've stopped hugging.

Too busy to realise they've become a business partnership, not a romantic one.

But it's fixable.

Because if you can survive night feeds, toddler tantrums, school admissions, and scraped knees…

You can survive the storm in your marriage.

You just have to turn toward each other again and remember:

Before you were "Mom and Dad,"
you were "Us."

Chapter 13: Parenthood – The Unspoken Strain

They say having a child brings couples closer.
Sometimes it does.
But often, it drives a silent wedge between them.

Not because of the child,
But because of everything that comes with becoming parents:

- Sleep deprivation
- Financial stress
- Hormonal changes
- Emotional burnout
- Shifting identities
- Different parenting philosophies
- Lack of intimacy
- Vanishing couple time

Over time, you're no longer lovers or partners.
You're co-managers of a high-stakes daycare.

When the Baby Arrives, the Marriage Changes

The birth of a child often births:

- A mother who feels overwhelmed and invisible

- A father who feels neglected or displaced
- Grandparents who interfere under the guise of "helping"
- Expectations that nobody prepared for

And in many cultures, the woman bears the brunt:

- Body changes
- Sleep loss
- Breastfeeding pain
- Career sacrifice
- Judgment for every choice

If her partner doesn't see, support, or show up,
Resentment builds silently.

The Hidden Incompatibilities

Before the baby, no one discussed:

- Will we co-sleep or sleep train?
- Will we do equal night shifts?
- Will we use formula if breastfeeding fails?
- Will we use gentle parenting or discipline strictly?
- Will religion play a role in raising the child?
- Who takes time off when the child is sick?

And so begins the daily arguments:

"You never help."

"You're too soft."

"Don't talk like that in front of the baby."

"I feel like a single parent."

Loss That Destroys

Sometimes, the parenting strain isn't about the child being alive, but about the child being lost.

- Miscarriages
- Stillbirths
- Infant deaths
- Abortion decisions
- IVF failures

These devastate couples.
Not because they didn't love each other,
But because grief speaks in different languages.

One partner may shut down.
The other may need to talk.
One wants silence. The other, connection.
And in that mismatch, the marriage slowly fractures.

Postpartum Changes Are Real

Many marriages don't survive because they didn't understand postpartum.

- Postpartum depression (PPD) isn't just sadness, it's detachment, anxiety, numbness.
- Hormonal shifts can last months to years.
- Some women lose libido completely. Others fear being touched.
- And yet, partners often think it's personal, "She's not attracted to me anymore."

Without education, empathy, and therapy, this becomes a breeding ground for:

- Affairs
- Loneliness
- Blame
- Divorce

When Parenting Styles Clash

- One is strict, the other indulgent
- One wants the child to be independent, the other protective
- One believes in spanking, the other finds it abusive
- One prioritises academics, the other emotional intelligence

The problem?
Children notice.
And they learn to play one parent against the other.

The real damage, though, is to the marriage,

Because you start parenting against each other instead of with each other.

Financial Tension

Children are expensive:

- Diapers, clothes, toys
- Daycare or nannies
- School fees, extracurriculars
- Medical emergencies
- Birthday parties, tuition, gadgets

Add to this:

- One partner sacrificing career momentum
- The other feeling sole pressure to provide
- Different views on spending vs saving

And suddenly, love drowns in Excel sheets and blame.

"We Stayed for the Kids" – But at What Cost?

Many couples stay unhappily married for the sake of children. They tell themselves:

"At least we're giving them a stable home."

But children see:

- Silent dinners
- Cold shoulders
- Arguments behind closed doors
- A mother who's always crying
- A father who's never around
- A home that feels heavy

Sometimes, a peaceful separation is more stable than a hostile marriage.

Reconnecting Through Parenthood

If you want to rebuild:

- Acknowledge the change. Your marriage needs new rules now.
- Appreciate each other. Say thank you for the small things.
- Prioritise time alone. Even 20 minutes a week to just talk without children.
- Go to therapy. Parenting stress deserves professional space.
- Check in weekly. "How are you feeling as a parent?" is a powerful question.

And always remember
You were partners before you were parents.
That bond needs watering too.

Chapter 14: The Cost of Keeping It Together

Marriage isn't what it used to be.

It's no longer about just emotional compatibility, it's about financial resilience.
Because modern marriages aren't only tested by feelings…
they're tested by EMIs, rising costs, school fees, insurance premiums, rent, groceries, medical emergencies, and constant comparison.

Couples don't just ask:

"Do we still love each other?"
They ask:
"Can we afford to stay together?"

And when every day feels like a financial firefight, love begins to feel like a luxury.

The Everyday Financial Avalanche

Most couples today aren't splurging recklessly.
They're simply trying to survive:

- Rent or home loan
- School fees
- Medical insurance

- Utility bills
- Car maintenance
- Groceries and basic child care
- Inflation on every front

Add to that:

- The pressure of maintaining a social image
- Vacation envy from social media
- Lifestyle expectations from extended family

And suddenly, the house that once held hope is now a stress factory.

The Mental Load of Money

What many people don't realise is:
Money isn't just practical, it's emotional.

Who's thinking about:

- Whether there's enough left for groceries?
- How to handle unexpected expenses?
- Whether the school fee deadline has passed?
- If there's savings for emergencies or a second child?

Usually, one partner carries the mental burden more than the other.

And when that emotional load goes unshared, resentment builds quietly.

School Fees vs. Couple Therapy

In a world where:

- Daycares cost like college,
- Tutors are non-negotiable,
- And branded water bottles are a status symbol in school…

…couples start cutting back, not on expenses, but on each other:

- "We can't afford a date night."
- "We'll talk later. I'm too tired."
- "Therapy's expensive, we'll manage."
- "We'll go on that trip someday."

Someday becomes never.

And the marriage becomes a ledger of postponed joy and hidden debt, both emotional and financial.

Two Incomes, Zero Breathing Room

Even with dual incomes, many couples feel broke.

Why?

- Because expenses scale with earnings
- Because ambition turns into burnout
- Because kids, home loans, and EMIs don't pause for mental health

They bought the house, the car, the school admission, the life…
But somewhere in that life, they lost the actual living.

And now, they stay, not because they're thriving, but because breaking up seems even more expensive.

Financial Stress Kills Intimacy

When you're worried about:

- Paying the next EMI
- Whether the credit card will go through
- If the kid's dental bill will derail this month's plan
- Or how to manage rising groceries on a shrinking budget

…it becomes incredibly hard to:

- Flirt
- Initiate sex
- Laugh freely
- Talk openly
- Feel safe
- Feel seen

Stress makes survival the priority.
And survival leaves no room for softness.

Keeping Up With… Everyone

Social media is silently dictating how couples live.
Not directly, but through subtle emotional pressure:

- "They just bought a bigger house."
- "Their vacation looked so perfect."
- "Their kid is in an international school."
- "Why don't we have that?"

Even if neither partner says it out loud, this pressure turns into:

- Overspending
- Overcommitting
- Compensating
- And silently blaming each other for not "providing more"

The marriage becomes a race.
And no one remembers why they started running.

What You Don't Say, Still Hurts

Many couples never say:

- "I'm scared we won't make it."
- "I'm drowning in pressure."

- "I feel like a failure."
- "I'm tired of acting like everything's okay."

Instead, they say:

- "Don't talk about it now."
- "You wouldn't understand."
- "We'll figure it out."

And slowly, they stop leaning on each other and start leaning away.

How to Stop Money from Ruining the Marriage

- Create a transparent monthly budget, not just on paper, but as a shared agreement.
- Split responsibilities, emotional and financial, not just bills.
- Talk money weekly, short check-ins reduce future explosions.
- Stop hiding debt or stress, it always shows up elsewhere.
- Cut out "status expenses", they don't impress the people who actually matter.
- Invest in your relationship like you invest in your child's tuition, dates, therapy, joy.
- Celebrate small wins, they're your real wealth.

Ask Each Other

- "What's our biggest financial fear right now?"
- "Do you feel alone in managing expenses?"
- "Are we building toward peace or just surviving chaos?"
- "Is our lifestyle hurting our love?"
- "What's one thing we can simplify together?"

Peace Is the New Luxury

In a world obsessed with more,
a calm home, a shared laugh, and emotional safety are priceless.

If money is pushing you apart, stop and ask:

"Are we spending so much energy earning, that we forgot what
we were earning for?"

Because the cost of keeping it together shouldn't be your
happiness.
And the cost of looking successful should never be your soul.

Chapter 15: Gender Wars & Role Confusion

We've come a long way.
Women work, earn, lead, and choose.
Men cry, nurture, co-parent, and question power.

It's progress.
But inside marriages, this shift has created something no one prepared us for: role confusion.

"Who's supposed to lead?"
"Who's supposed to adjust?"
"Who sacrifices what and when?"
"What does being a good husband or wife even mean anymore?"

This chapter explores how evolving gender expectations are colliding with outdated conditioning, and how the result is not freedom, but frustration.

Equality Without Instruction

We all agree now:

- Marriage should be equal.
- Both partners should contribute.
- No one should dominate or disappear.

But what does "equal" actually look like in daily life?

- Who wakes up for the baby?
- Who handles the money?
- Who calls the plumber or repairs the car?
- Who cooks?
- Who compromises during a relocation or career pivot?

Equality is a beautiful principle, but without conversations, it becomes a source of tension.

The Pressure on Women: Do Everything. Be Everything.

Today's women are told:

- Be independent, but soft.
- Be ambitious, but family-first.
- Look good, but don't try too hard.
- Earn, nurture, plan, host, raise, love and don't complain.

In marriage, this turns into:

- Managing a career and a household
- Being blamed for being "too busy"
- Being shamed for being "too dependent"
- Getting judged by in-laws for not doing things "the traditional way"
- Feeling torn between personal dreams and invisible expectations

And often, the man says he supports her…
But the housework, child-rearing, and emotional labor still fall on her plate.

The Pressure on Men: Provide, Protect, Pretend You're Fine.

Men, too, are stuck in a painful place.

They're told:

- Share your feelings, but don't be weak.
- Respect her ambition, but don't feel insecure.
- Be soft, but strong.
- Be available, but earn like a machine.

In marriage, this becomes:

- Suppressing emotions to appear "stable"
- Feeling replaced when their partner succeeds
- Feeling attacked when she demands equality
- Not knowing how to express stress without sounding like a failure

Many men feel emotionally inadequate, but can't admit it.
So they withdraw. Or become defensive. Or lash out.
Not out of dominance, but out of confusion.

Feminism Misunderstood, Masculinity Misused

Feminism isn't the enemy.

It's the reason so many women now have voice, choice, and financial freedom.

But in many homes, feminism is misunderstood as:

- "She doesn't need a man."
- "She's too controlling."
- "She wants to be the boss."
- "She wants all the benefits with none of the responsibilities."

On the other side, traditional masculinity often shows up as:

- "I pay, so I decide."
- "I'm supposed to lead, not ask."
- "If I show emotion, I'll lose respect."
- "I'm not built for emotional drama."

Both extremes hurt marriages.

What's needed now is new language. New roles. New rules.

Redefining Partnership, Not Power Struggles

The healthiest modern marriages aren't about:

- Keeping score
- Competing
- Outsmarting

They're about:

- Flexibility
- Communication
- Shared purpose

Roles are not fixed, they're fluid.
The one who earns more today might take a step back tomorrow.
The one who stays home today might return to work next year.
The one who cooks now might take on finances later.

It's not about who does what, it's about how you decide together.

When Roles Become Weapons

In many troubled marriages, role expectations are weaponised:

- "I work all day, you can at least cook."
- "You're the man. Step up."
- "You wanted feminism. Why are you crying now?"
- "You earn less, so stay quiet."
- "I do more. I matter more."

This power-play turns love into a hierarchy.

And the partnership begins to feel like a competition no one can win.

Healing the Role Rift

- Have the hard conversations. Who does what, why, and how often?
- Check for invisible labor. Who's carrying the mental load, scheduling, planning, worrying?
- Don't mock each other's struggles. Both career and housework are valid stressors.
- Celebrate role reversals. If he stays home or she earns more, normalise it.
- Share success. If one wins, both rise.
- Let go of shame. If you're feeling lost, talk, not fight.

Ask Each Other

- "Do you feel valued for what you bring to this marriage?"
- "Have you ever felt forced into a role you didn't want?"
- "What would equality look like to you?"
- "Do you feel safe showing weakness to me?"
- "What roles can we redefine together?"

The Goal Is Balance, Not Symmetry

You don't need to split everything 50/50.
You need to split it in a way that feels fair, supportive, and fluid.

Some weeks you'll give 80, some weeks 20.
Some days you'll lead, some days you'll follow.
But both of you should feel seen, heard, and free to evolve.

Because gender roles were meant to be tools, not chains.

And in a marriage of equals, the most powerful sentence is:

"Let's figure this out together."

Chapter 16: Mental Health & Marital Burnout

It starts slowly.

You forget to laugh together.
You avoid eye contact at breakfast.
You both scroll in silence, lying side by side.
Fights have become either daily or non-existent, and somehow,
both feel worse.

There's no drama.
No cheating.
No screaming.

Just… exhaustion.

Welcome to marital burnout, the silent killer of modern
relationships.

What Is Marital Burnout?

It's not about hating your partner.
It's about being too drained to care.

- You go through the motions but feel disconnected.
- You try to have conversations, but they turn into chores.
- You think of solving problems, but your brain whispers:
  "What's the point?"

Marital burnout is a mix of:

- Chronic stress
- Emotional depletion
- Unspoken resentment
- Repetitive disappointment
- And the lack of emotional safety

And often, it hides behind a busy schedule, a smiling selfie, or a child's PTA meeting.

When Mental Health Enters the Chat

Most couples don't realise that:

- Anxiety can make your partner irritable, not cruel.
- Depression can make them distant, not disinterested.
- Burnout can make you numb, not unloving.
- Childhood trauma can make communication feel unsafe.
- Postpartum changes can redefine intimacy.
- Unhealed grief can create unexplained silence.

But because mental health is rarely discussed in marriages, these challenges often get misinterpreted as:

- Laziness
- Coldness
- Selfishness
- Rejection

- Or "not trying hard enough"

And that misunderstanding becomes the actual crack in the foundation.

Signs You're in a Burnt-Out Marriage

- Conversations feel like obligations
- Physical intimacy feels absent, forced, or one-sided
- You fantasise about "freedom," not cheating
- Every day feels like survival, not partnership
- One or both partners feel emotionally invisible
- You're constantly "fine", but never really okay
- Even kindness feels like effort

You're not just tired.
You're tired of being tired.

The Silence That Hurts More Than Screaming

In a burned-out marriage, silence becomes a survival tool:

- "Let's not talk about it."
- "It'll just become a fight."
- "He won't get it."
- "She's already stressed."
- "I'll just deal with it."

But this silence slowly eats away at:

- Trust
- Intimacy
- Curiosity
- Playfulness
- Partnership

And soon, you're two people managing a life together, but not living it together.

"I Can't Be Your Therapist"

Here's the tricky part.
Your partner is your safe space, but they are not your sole source of healing.

When one partner is deeply struggling with mental health, the other may feel:

- Drained
- Helpless
- Trapped
- Unseen

Yes, you should be supportive.
Yes, you should care.

But you also need your own oxygen mask.

Because marriages collapse when one person becomes the caregiver, and the other becomes the patient, permanently.

Steps to Reignite the Burnt-Out Bond

- Name it. Say, "I think we're burnt out." Language gives clarity.
- Prioritise therapy. Not as a last resort, but as a maintenance tool.
- Take solo time. Space is not distance. It's healing.
- Revisit your 'why'. Why did you marry? What still matters?
- Redefine intimacy. Start with emotional safety before sexual healing.
- Stop blaming. Replace "you never…" with "can we try…"
- Celebrate micro-moments. A shared cup of tea. A kind text. A deep breath together.

These small rituals are emotional CPR.

Therapy Is Not a Threat

Going to couples therapy doesn't mean:

- You've failed
- You're weak
- You're on the edge of divorce

It means:

You care enough to try, even when it's hard.

A therapist doesn't take sides.
They translate pain into understanding.
They help you hear each other again.

And sometimes, they help you grieve what the marriage used to be, so you can build what it can still become.

Ask Yourselves

- "When did we last feel like a team?"
- "Do we still know each other's dreams?"
- "Are we avoiding conflict or avoiding connection?"
- "Do I feel emotionally safe here?"
- "Is this marriage taking care of me or just taking from me?"

You're Allowed to Heal, Together

Burnout isn't the end.
It's a signal.
A cry.
A warning light that says: you've driven too far without pausing to refuel.

You don't have to give up.
You don't have to stay stuck either.

You can pause.

Rest.
Talk.
Rebuild.

Because love isn't just found at the start of the journey.
Sometimes, the deepest love is found when you choose to stay
and repair… together.

Part III: The Breaking Point and Beyond

Chapter 17: The Fantasy of "Better Out There"

There's a dangerous whisper in the modern world.

"You could do better."
"You deserve more."
"Someone out there will love you the way they don't."
"Just one swipe… and you'll see."

It starts subtly. A moment of boredom. A fight that leaves a scar. A phase of loneliness in your marriage.
And then that whisper grows louder, fed by friends, apps, influencers, and the endless scroll of curated happiness.

Suddenly, the person you once loved starts to feel… average.
And the idea of "better out there" becomes seductive.

The Tinder Generation of Discontent

Swipe culture has rewritten our brains.
We now live in a world of:

- Infinite options
- Zero patience
- Comparison overload
- Fantasy over reality
- Attention over intention

In this world, people aren't just people.
They're profiles.
Filtered, packaged, available.

And marriage, a slow, demanding, real commitment, feels
outdated when novelty is one click away.

The Grass Is Greener Syndrome

You begin to believe:

- Other couples are happier
- Other spouses are more understanding
- Other relationships are more fun, sexy, exciting
- Your marriage is too heavy, boring, or "past its prime"

But here's the truth:

The grass is greener where you water it.

Most relationships hit dry seasons.
And instead of irrigating what we have, we often look over the
fence, forgetting that even the most beautiful lawn needs tending.

The Role of Social Media

Instagram and reels have normalised:

- Public affection

- Grand gestures
- Exotic vacations
- Spouses dancing together, glowing together, building empires together

What we don't see:

- The arguments before the vacation
- The silence after the shoot
- The resentment behind the ring
- The therapy between posts

Comparison creates disillusionment.
It tells you, "Other marriages are effortless. Yours is broken."
But effortlessness is an illusion.
Behind every beautiful moment is invisible work.

Emotional Affairs Begin with Curiosity

It starts innocently:

- A late-night text from a friend.
- A "like" that leads to a conversation.
- A work buddy who seems to understand you.
- A stranger who "gets" you more than your spouse seems to.

You tell yourself: "It's just talking."
But soon, you're confiding more in them than in your partner.

And once emotional intimacy shifts, the foundation of your marriage begins to crack.

Not all affairs are physical.
Many begin in the mind.
But they destroy marriages all the same.

What If You Really Could Find Someone Better?

Maybe you could.

Maybe someone out there is:

- More attractive
- More successful
- More emotionally intelligent
- More sexually compatible

But even they will eventually disappoint you.
Because every relationship becomes real.
And real means:
- Boring routines
- Unmet expectations
- Conflicts
- Healing from pasts
- Growth that isn't always parallel

And if your belief is "the right person won't need this much work,"
you'll keep changing partners instead of changing patterns.

What Does "Better" Even Mean?

Better is not:

- More expensive dates
- More compliments
- A better body or smoother sex

Better is:

- Feeling safe during conflict
- Being seen on your worst day
- Knowing someone chooses you, even when it's hard
- Growing through life's changes without growing apart

That doesn't happen by accident.
It happens when people choose love again and again, even after the excitement fades.

Ask Yourself Honestly

- "Am I comparing my real life to someone else's highlight reel?"
- "Am I avoiding tough conversations by fantasising about escape?"

- "Is my dissatisfaction rooted in neglect or unmet fantasies?"
- "Would I rather fix something or start over every time it gets hard?"
- "Do I truly want someone new or do I just want this person to see me again?"

When Is It Not Just a Phase?

Sometimes the fantasy of better out there isn't just a phase, it's a signal:

- You've emotionally outgrown the relationship
- You've been neglected, disrespected, or abused
- You've tried everything and are living like strangers
- You feel more alive outside the marriage than within

If that's the case, your desire to leave may not be fantasy.
It may be clarity.

But if you're chasing "better" without examining why you're dissatisfied, you may be escaping yourself, not your marriage.

How to Return to Reality and Reconnect

- **Pause the fantasy**. Don't make decisions in a fog of comparison.
- **Talk**. Ask your spouse: "Do you feel like we're drifting?"
- **Rebuild rituals**. Date nights, deep talks, shared goals.

- **Unfollow toxic content**. If it makes you resent your life, it's not harmless.
- **Choose curiosity**. What do you not know about your partner anymore? Rediscover them.
- **Seek therapy**. Even if things aren't broken, especially then.

You Can Want More, Without Wanting Someone Else

Wanting growth, romance, laughter, and passion is natural.
But these don't always live elsewhere.
Sometimes, they're buried right where you are, under routine, wounds, and silence.

Dig deep.
Water the roots.
And remember: real love doesn't look like a fantasy.
It looks like work, wonder, forgiveness, and choice.

Chapter 18: When Friends Sabotage Marriages

Friendship is supposed to be a source of strength during marriage.
A safe space to vent.
A place to be heard without being judged.
A circle that protects, not poisons.

But in today's world, where opinions are broadcasted like facts and boundaries often blur, friends can quietly sabotage a marriage without even realising it.

Or worse, some do it knowingly.

The "Support" That Isn't Support

You had a bad fight.
You're emotional.
You call your friend.

And before you've even finished explaining, they say:

- "I don't know how you put up with this."
- "If I were you, I'd leave."
- "This is not how a man should treat a woman."
- "Don't be a doormat. You deserve better."
- "Why is she always so controlling?"

They may mean well.

But their support often comes with biased advice, fuelled by their own baggage.

Because friends:

- Project their own traumas
- Remember only your worst moments
- Don't live your everyday life, they see the highlight reels you present
- Rarely know both sides of the story

In trying to defend you, they may teach you to defend yourself from your own spouse.

When Party Culture Replaces Partnership

In many urban friend circles, marriage becomes the odd one out.

If your friend group is mostly single, partying, or career-focused, they might:

- Encourage reckless independence
- Downplay your partner's role in your life
- Roll their eyes when you skip late nights for family time
- Make jokes about how "married people are boring"

They may not sabotage you deliberately.
But they slowly shift your mindset from commitment to escapism.

And that shift grows louder when:

- They push you to flirt, just for "fun"
- They say, "One drink won't hurt, don't tell him"
- They suggest, "Everyone cheats a little, don't be so uptight"

Emotional Affairs Begin with "Just Friends"

Another trap: the friend of the opposite sex (or someone you're attracted to) who's "just really easy to talk to."

You tell yourself:

- "They get me."
- "They're just a good listener."
- "I need someone who understands."

But slowly:

- You begin to emotionally rely on them more than your spouse
- You start hiding the closeness
- You share things you no longer tell your partner

And that's no longer friendship.
That's emotional replacement.

When Friends Feed Your Insecurities

Some friends say things like:

- "You've changed since you got married."
- "You don't dress like you used to."
- "You used to be so ambitious."
- "I don't know if he really deserves you."
- "She's lucky you even stayed."

What they're really saying is:

"Don't grow in ways I can't relate to anymore."

And their subtle jabs make you:

- Doubt your worth
- Resent your partner
- Long for your past self
- Question your choices

True friends help you evolve with your marriage, not against it.

Friends Who Secretly Want You to Fail

It's rare, but it happens.

Some friends:

- Are bitter about their own failed relationships
- Are jealous of your bond

- Enjoy the drama
- Want to be the centre of your attention again
- Harbour unresolved attraction to you

And so they:

- Plant doubts
- Exaggerate flaws
- Undermine your partner
- Create unnecessary suspicion
- Say things like, "Are you sure he's not cheating?" without evidence

This isn't friendship.
It's sabotage, dressed in empathy.

How to Protect Your Marriage Without Cutting Friends Off

You don't have to isolate yourself.
But you must curate your influences.

Set boundaries:

- "I'm not looking for advice, just a listener."
- "I need support for my marriage, not fuel against it."
- "Let's not talk about my partner behind their back."
- "If you only hear one side, please don't judge us."

Recalibrate:

- Share more with people who support growth, not drama
- Limit discussions about marital conflict to trusted, balanced voices
- Involve a therapist when needed, not a gossip group chat

Questions to Ask Yourself

- "Does this friend make me a better spouse or a more bitter one?"
- "Do I find myself hiding how much I complain to them?"
- "Are they rooting for my marriage or just for me to 'be free'?"
- "Would I be okay if my spouse had a friendship like this?"

Choose Your Circle with Intention

A good friend:

- Wants your marriage to succeed
- Supports you without bias
- Reminds you of your own power
- Encourages communication, not escape
- Doesn't treat your spouse like the enemy

Marriages are hard enough.

Surround yourself with people who hold your vows with the same care you do.

Chapter 19: The "Roommate Syndrome"

They share a home.
They share bills.
They raise kids.
They sometimes share a bed.

But emotionally, mentally, and spiritually, they're miles apart.

This is the quietest kind of heartbreak:

When you're not fighting, but you're not close.
When the love isn't gone, but the connection is.
When your spouse feels more like a co-parent, flatmate, or teammate… than a partner.

This is Roommate Syndrome.

And it's become one of the most common and undetected causes of unhappy marriages.

How It Starts

It rarely begins with drama.

It begins with:

- Busy workdays
- Tired evenings

- Parenting fatigue
- Repeating routines
- Unresolved arguments that fade instead of heal
- Emotional needs not expressed (or not heard)
- Physical affection slowing down
- Time together shrinking to minutes

And suddenly, the person who once made your heart race now barely makes your pulse change.

Life Becomes Logistics

You talk, but only about:

- Groceries
- School meetings
- Who's paying the electricity bill
- Who's picking up the kid
- What's for dinner

You live in the same house, but you're living separate emotional lives.

You may not even be angry. Just… flat.

No passion. No play. No curiosity. No spark.
Just comfort mixed with mild resentment.
Like worn-out furniture that you never get around to replacing.

Signs You've Become Roommates

- You no longer hug or kiss just because
- You don't miss each other when apart
- You watch separate shows in separate rooms
- Conversations are short, transactional
- You can't remember the last deep talk
- You're more excited about being alone than being together
- You've stopped having sex or it feels mechanical
- You both feel like you're doing it "for the kids"

It doesn't feel toxic.
It just feels… distant.

And the worst part? You're not even sure when it happened.

Why It Hurts So Deeply

Because you're grieving something you still technically have.

They're there.
They're not cruel.
They're not abusive.
They're just… not with you anymore.

And this limbo is more suffocating than separation.

You wonder:

- "Is this what marriage becomes?"
- "Is it selfish to want more?"
- "Should I stay for stability, or leave for aliveness?"

The Role of Emotional Neglect

People assume abuse destroys marriages.
But often, it's neglect that causes the quiet collapse.

Neglect doesn't mean malice.
It means:

- Not checking in
- Not noticing subtle needs
- Not making time
- Not being present

And in long marriages, this often isn't due to lack of love,
but lack of maintenance.

Rebuilding from Roommate Mode

It's not easy. But it's possible.

Step 1: Acknowledge the drift.
Say it. Out loud. Kindly.

"I feel like we're growing apart and I miss you."

Step 2: Recreate rituals.
Bring back date nights.
Schedule device-free dinners.
Start a shared hobby.
Take walks together.

Step 3: Stop waiting for 'the mood'.
Desire and connection are often built through action, not before it.

Step 4: Ask better questions.
Not "How was your day?"
Ask: "What made you laugh today?" or "Is there something
you're excited about lately?"

Step 5: Touch again.
Non-sexual affection matters. A hand on the back. A gentle hug.
Relearning how to be tender.

Step 6: Get help if needed.
There is no shame in couples therapy. It's not a sign of failure, it's
a sign of investment.

Questions to Ask Each Other

- "Do you feel like we're emotionally close these days?"
- "What's one thing you wish we did more often?"
- "When did we feel most 'us'?"
- "What made you fall in love with me and do I still show
  you that part of myself?"

- "Can we rebuild, not who we were, but who we want to become together?"

If You're Already Checked Out…

Sometimes, you've tried.
And nothing changes.
The other person isn't interested in reconnecting.
Or they don't even acknowledge that anything is wrong.

In such cases, staying becomes emotional starvation.

If you feel:

- Unseen
- Tired of trying
- Unheard
- Empty for too long

It may be time to ask yourself:

"Am I keeping this marriage alive… or is it already over and I'm just maintaining the corpse?"

Partnership Is More Than Proximity

Living under one roof does not mean living as one team.
If your marriage has slipped into roommate mode, it doesn't mean it's doomed.

But it does mean it's time to act.

Connection must be created again and again.
Not with grand gestures, but with daily presence.

Because you didn't get married to co-exist.
You got married to co-live.

Chapter 20: Why "Trying" Isn't Enough

Every time a marriage begins to fall apart, someone says:

"But I'm trying."
"We've both been trying."
"We gave it everything."
"Isn't that enough?"

And yes, trying matters.
But not all "trying" leads to healing.

Because you can try the wrong things,
you can try for the wrong reasons,
you can try alone,
and you can try to hold on to something that should be let go.

Effort Doesn't Equal Intimacy

You can:

- Cook dinner every night
- Pay all the bills
- Plan holidays
- Stay loyal
- Do chores
- Be "nice"

…and still have a partner who feels unloved.

Why?

Because marriage isn't a checklist.
It's a connection.

Effort without emotional investment is like wrapping a gift with no present inside.

It looks good, but feels hollow.

Trying Can Become a Repeating Loop

Many couples fall into a pattern:

- Things feel broken
- One person "tries" to change
- The other softens, briefly
- The old behaviour returns
- The resentment deepens
- Repeat

This kind of trying burns people out.

It's not trying to grow,
It's trying to postpone the inevitable.

Are You Trying or Just Performing?

Sometimes we try:

- To look like the better person
- To avoid guilt
- To make our parents proud
- To keep the kids happy
- To stop being "the one who gave up"
- Because we're afraid to be alone

But all that trying is external.
It doesn't come from a deep desire to reconnect.
It comes from fear, pressure, or ego.

And when that's the fuel, you'll run out fast.

Trying to Change the Other Person

This is the most exhausting form of trying:

"If only they listened more."
"If they just went for therapy."
"If they stopped lying."
"If they worked less."
"If they were more romantic."

So you try to fix, to teach, to wait.

And they?
Stay exactly the same.

Truth is:

- You cannot try for someone.
- You cannot drag someone to intimacy.
- You cannot force someone to grow.

You can invite. Inspire. Lead.
But they have to want it too.

Sometimes, You're Not Trying the Right Way

Trying harder is not always the answer.
Sometimes you need to try differently.

Instead of:

Talking louder → try listening deeper
Doing more chores → try asking what truly matters to them
Offering solutions → try sitting in their pain without fixing
Demanding change → try showing your own vulnerability

Effort is not the same as empathy.
And doing everything except what they actually need is still a
form of avoidance.

Trying When the Foundation Is Broken

Some things cannot be "tried" away:

- Addictions that are untreated
- Abuse, emotional or physical

- Repeated betrayals
- Values that don't align
- Total emotional shutdown
- Incompatibility around children, religion, lifestyle
- Ongoing disrespect

Trying in these cases becomes self-destruction.

You're not saving the marriage.
You're sacrificing yourself to keep up appearances.

And in doing so, you abandon your own sanity and self-worth.

Try with Intention, Not Just Repetition

If you're going to try, ask:

- "What am I trying for?"
- "Do we want the same future?"
- "Is this effort mutual?"
- "Are we rebuilding, or just replaying the past?"
- "Am I losing myself in the process?"

What Effective Trying Looks Like

- Trying to listen, not just reply
- Trying to understand how they feel safe
- Trying to speak your needs without blame
- Trying new tools, books, therapy, couple's workshops

- Trying to see yourself as they experience you
- Trying to let go of ego and old patterns
- Trying together, not alone

When Letting Go Is the Bravest Try of All

Sometimes, real effort looks like this:

- Accepting that you've changed
- Admitting it's not working
- Releasing someone you love
- Choosing peace over pretending
- Ending it with kindness, not cruelty

Trying to stay is not always heroic.
Sometimes, the real courage is in knowing when it's time to stop.

Because your energy is sacred.
And love shouldn't be about who can "hold on the longest."
It should be about who can grow the deepest and choose with
clarity.

Chapter 21: Sacred Differences – When Belief Divides Instead of Unites

When two people fall in love, religion often takes a backseat. Rituals can seem irrelevant. Customs, optional. Faith, flexible.

But marriage?
Marriage makes everything real.
It pulls in families, traditions, festivals, children and suddenly, belief isn't background noise anymore.
It's loud, loaded, and unmissable.

Faith Was Never Just Private

No matter how modern a couple may be, marriage brings pressure to:

- Celebrate religious festivals with a certain decorum
- Follow rituals (weddings, funerals, housewarmings) "properly"
- Name or raise children in a specific religious framework
- Eat, dress, or live according to inherited customs
- Stay "true" to their roots, especially in the eyes of extended family

One partner may say, "Why can't you just respect my culture?"
The other may say, "Why do I have to follow what I don't believe in?"

And love, once carefree, becomes conditional.
Because religion isn't just belief, it's identity, family, loyalty.

When Culture Clashes with Compatibility

Sometimes it's not about religion itself, but cultural expectations tied to it:

- Gender roles (e.g., women must fast for husbands, men must lead prayers)
- Clothing rules (e.g., modesty, coverings, shaving)
- Food taboos (e.g., no beef, no pork, no alcohol, only vegetarian kitchens)
- Parenting disagreements (e.g., should kids go to temple/mosque/church?)
- Financial giving (e.g., tithes, donations to religious bodies)

One sees it as devotion.
The other sees it as pressure.
And suddenly, faith becomes friction.

Silent Conversions and Hidden Resentments

In many societies, people marry into faiths they don't belong to because of:

- Family pressure
- Legal ease (in interfaith countries)
- Social acceptance

- The assumption that "it's just paperwork" or "symbolic"

But inside:

- One partner mourns the slow erasure of their identity
- The other feels isolated when their rituals aren't respected
- Children grow up confused or burdened with divided loyalties

This creates unspoken resentments that often emerge years later, during a family crisis, a funeral, or a naming ceremony.

What We Don't Talk About

Love stories rarely mention:

- The partner who pretends to fast, but secretly eats
- The one who sits through rituals they don't believe in just to keep peace
- The couple who skips festivals altogether to avoid fights
- The loneliness of feeling like a foreigner in your own home
- The tension when raising a child between two belief systems

These aren't dramatic issues, but they are slowly erosive ones.

And they create a home full of politeness, but no peace.

Can Interfaith Marriages Work?

Yes, when done consciously.
Here's what helps:

1. Radical Honesty (Before Marriage)

Ask and answer:

- "Which rituals matter to you?"
- "What will we teach our kids?"
- "How much do your parents expect?"
- "Are you okay not converting, or if I don't?"

2. Mutual Respect (After Marriage)

Respect doesn't mean participating in everything.
It means not mocking, shaming, or dismissing the other's beliefs.
It also means allowing space for opt-outs without guilt.

3. Unified Parenting

You must agree on:

- What's taught at home
- What's allowed at school or temple/mosque
- What holidays are celebrated and how

Confused children become anxious adults.

4. Community Boundaries

You're not marrying their entire community.

So you get to decide how involved you want to be and what's off-limits.

When It's No Longer Tolerable

Sometimes, it doesn't work out:

- When one partner becomes more radical after marriage
- When families start interfering and insisting
- When rituals feel forced, or disrespect becomes normalised
- When the pressure to convert, raise children a certain way, or abandon your own beliefs becomes non-negotiable

At that point, staying might mean abandoning who you are. And that's a cost no love should ask you to pay.

Faith Should Deepen Love, Not Divide It

In the best marriages:

- Faith is shared, or at least supported
- Differences are acknowledged, not erased
- Children grow up with clarity and choice
- Couples become stronger, not in spite of their differences, but because of how they hold them gently

You don't have to believe the same things. But you must believe in each other, deeply, respectfully, and with compassion.

Because a marriage of mismatched faiths can still thrive,
if love becomes the highest shared religion.

Chapter 22: Living with Their Demons – Addiction and the Marriage That Bleeds

No one marries thinking they'll end up hiding alcohol bottles.

Or smelling their partner's breath at 8 a.m.

Or paying off secret debts.

Or crying themselves to sleep after another broken promise.

Addiction doesn't just destroy the addict.

It drains the partner.

It poisons the home.

It turns love into constant crisis management.

Addiction Comes in Many Forms

It's not always alcohol or drugs.

It can be:

- Gambling
- Pornography
- Gaming
- Food
- Prescription meds
- Even workaholism or obsessive spending

And what begins as a coping mechanism slowly becomes:

A monster that needs feeding every day.

The Invisible Damage

The addicted partner often says:

"It's my problem, not yours."

But they're wrong.

Because addiction affects:

- Trust
- Finances
- Emotional safety
- Physical intimacy
- Parenting consistency
- Daily peace

And the non-addicted partner becomes:

- The fixer
- The secret-keeper
- The caretaker
- The emotional punching bag

Or worse…
The co-addict, someone who enables, excuses, and covers up.

🧯 Living in Survival Mode

Every day is unpredictable.

Will they be sober today?
Will they come home?
Will they remember what they said last night?

You live:

- On edge
- On alert
- On empty

You plan less. Dream less. Hope less.

And slowly, you lose yourself.

Love Is Not Enough

Many partners stay because:

- "They weren't always like this"
- "They need me"
- "It's just a phase"
- "What if they relapse if I leave?"

But here's the truth:

You can't love someone out of addiction.
You can only support them if they're willing to walk out of it themselves.

Warning Signs You're Losing Yourself

- You lie to their boss, friends, or family
- You cover up bruises or damage
- You make excuses for their behaviour
- You've stopped asking for what you need
- You cry in private but act fine in public
- You've stopped trusting your own judgment

This isn't "standing by your partner."
This is slow suicide.

What Recovery Looks Like

Recovery doesn't mean they "say sorry" or promise to stop.
It means:

- Professional help: rehab, therapy, medication
- Real accountability: joining groups, checking in, transparent routines
- Long-term commitment: not just quitting, but healing
- Taking ownership: not blaming stress, childhood, or you

If these are not in place, you are not in recovery, you're in a loop.

When to Leave

Leave if:

- They refuse help
- They relapse repeatedly with no remorse
- They blame you for their addiction
- Your physical or mental health is at risk
- Your children are affected
- You've done all you can and nothing changes

Choosing yourself is not betrayal.
It's survival.

If They're Trying, and You Want to Stay

Then:

- Set clear boundaries: no abuse, no lying, no stealing
- Join support groups like Al-Anon
- Work with a couples therapist who understands addiction
- Prioritise your self-care. You can't pour from an empty cup.

Remember, relapse is part of recovery, but it can't become an excuse.

Love Without Rescue

You are not their parent, doctor, or saviour.

You are their partner.

Support them.
But never sacrifice your sanity to prove your loyalty.

Because in the end, a marriage haunted by addiction can only heal
if:

- The addict owns their recovery
- The partner owns their boundaries

You both must fight the demon.
But if only one of you is fighting, then it's not a marriage, it's a
war zone.

Chapter 23: Staying After the Storm – When Cheating Doesn't End the Marriage

When we think of cheating, we imagine:

A hotel room.
A secret text.
A kiss that shouldn't have happened.

But cheating isn't always physical.
It can be:

- An emotional affair that runs deeper than sex
- Late-night conversations filled with intimacy
- Secret apps and hidden social media messages
- Rekindled bonds with an ex
- Even watching porn compulsively while ignoring your partner

And yet, many couples stay together.

Why?

Because love doesn't always vanish with betrayal.
Sometimes, it's the start of a long, messy attempt to rebuild.

The Myth of "Once a Cheater…"

People love to say:

"Once a cheater, always a cheater."

But human behaviour isn't always so simple.

Sometimes:

- A faithful person cheats because they felt emotionally neglected
- A mistake leads to genuine remorse and transformation
- An affair becomes a mirror to deeper cracks in the relationship

Yes, cheating is a choice.
But not all cheating comes from evil.
Some comes from emptiness.

The Psychological Fallout

For the betrayed partner:

- Constant self-doubt: "Was I not enough?"
- Nightmares, panic attacks, rage
- Obsession with the details: "How many times?" "Where?" "Did you love them?"

- Hyper-vigilance and checking behaviour: passwords, phones, receipts
- Difficulty trusting, even after genuine change

For the partner who cheated:

- Shame and self-hate
- Guilt-driven overcompensation
- Feeling permanently judged
- Struggling to balance remorse with a plea for normalcy

Both are in pain.
Just different kinds.

Not All Marriages Can or Should Survive

Staying only because:

- "We have children"
- "I don't want to lose money"
- "What will people say?"
- "We've been together too long"

…is a slow death.

Because forgiveness is not the same as tolerance.

If the cheating partner:

- Minimises the affair
- Justifies it as your fault
- Keeps secrets or stays in touch with the third person
- Refuses therapy or honesty

Then you're not rebuilding.
You're reliving trauma.

But Some Marriages Become Stronger

Yes, really.

When both partners:

- Take full ownership (no blame-shifting)
- Are brutally honest
- Go through therapy
- Learn better communication tools
- Rebuild trust step-by-step
- Treat the relationship like a new beginning
- Work through the pain, not around it

Then the affair becomes not the end, but the wake-up call.

Ground Rules for Rebuilding After Infidelity

1.   Radical Transparency
All passwords, devices, schedules… open.
Not as control, but as rebuilding trust.

2.   No Contact with the Affair Partner

Zero. Ever again.

3.   Consistent Effort Over Time

Healing takes months, not weeks.

Relapses in trust are normal.

4.   Validation of Pain

"Get over it" is never an option.

Say: "I understand I hurt you. I will keep showing up."

5.   Therapy for Both

Together and separately.

What to Say (and What Not to)

Avoid saying:

- "It was just sex."
- "If you hadn't changed, I wouldn't have done it."
- "It didn't mean anything."
- "You should be over it by now."

Say instead:

- "I was wrong."
- "You didn't deserve this."
- "I'll answer any questions you need."
- "I want to earn your trust again."

And If You Can't Forgive?

That's okay.

Forgiveness is a choice. Not a duty.

If you:

- Can't stop imagining the betrayal
- Have lost all desire for intimacy
- Feel disgusted or disconnected
- No longer feel safe emotionally or physically

Then leaving is not failure.
It's self-respect.

Choosing Love After the Earthquake

If you stay, let it be because:

- You've both changed
- You're both healing
- You're both building a future, not dragging the past

Rebuilding doesn't erase the cracks.
But sometimes, the strongest marriages are those repaired with gold.

Chapter 24: When Work Comes Between Us – Career, Ambition, and the Marriage Drift

Love doesn't die overnight.
But it can starve in boardrooms, airport lounges, and unread messages.

Today's marriages don't collapse because someone fell out of love.
They collapse because there's no time, space, or alignment left to feed it.

And one of the biggest culprits?

Career ambition.

The Modern Dream: Partner, Parent, and Powerhouse

We grew up being told:

"You can have it all."

But no one warned us about:

- 14-hour workdays
- Multiple relocations

- Long-distance living
- Promotions that cost peace
- Job losses that shatter identity
- The silent competition between two working spouses
- Or the guilt that comes with every skipped family dinner

When One Rises and the Other Waits

Resentment grows in imbalance:

- She puts her career on hold for the baby. He gets promoted.
- He quits his job for her posting. She becomes distant.
- One travels the world. The other handles homework and groceries.
- One partner thrives, the other quietly disappears.

The worst part?
Neither is necessarily wrong.
But equality in marriage doesn't mean doing the same thing, it means carrying equal weight.

And when one person carries most of the emotional or domestic burden,
Even success begins to feel like betrayal.

Career vs. Connection

Many couples fall into these traps:

- Talking only about work, money, goals
- Treating the partner as a "sounding board," not a teammate
- Making major career decisions without consulting the other
- Expecting applause for success, but offering no space for struggle
- Believing that providing financially is enough

But even the richest marriage can feel emotionally bankrupt.

Because what we do isn't who we are.
And marriage needs presence, not just provision.

When Careers Pull You Apart Geographically

LDRs (Long Distance Relationships) are common now:

- International postings
- Onsite tech projects
- Cabin crew, merchant navy, touring artists, athletes

In theory: It's temporary. We'll adjust.
In reality:

- Calls shrink
- Time zones clash
- Loneliness creeps in
- And temptations or emotional gaps sneak up

Distance doesn't just test love.

It changes people.

And sometimes, they grow in opposite directions.

The Ego of Achievement

Sometimes, the real damage is pride:

"I earn more, so I get to decide."
"My job is more demanding."
"Your work isn't as serious as mine."
"You're lucky I'm doing all this for us."

Success warps humility.
And when one partner starts talking down to the other,
Respect erodes… fast.

No title is worth that cost.

The Psychology of Insecurity

When both partners are ambitious, another problem arises:

- Who's doing better?
- Who's more admired socially?
- Who's the "star" of the couple?

Subtle competition leads to:

- Undermining each other
- Passive-aggressive remarks
- Jealousy masked as indifference
- One-upmanship

You stop being each other's cheerleader.
And start being quiet rivals.

How to Keep Love Alive Amid Ambition

1.   Choose Alignment Over Surprise
Big career decisions should be joint conversations, not announcements.

2.   Celebrate Both Journeys
Your startup, her PhD, his transfer, her sabbatical, all matter.

3.   Make Time Non-Negotiable
Even 30 minutes a day with full attention is better than hours of distraction.

4.   Redefine Success Together
What does "making it" mean? A house? Time with kids? Peace? Align definitions.

5.   Never Weaponise Money or Titles
The moment you do, the marriage becomes a job interview.

If One Partner Feels Left Behind

Say it.
Don't swallow it.

And the other partner must not get defensive.
Instead of "You're just jealous,"
Say: "I can see how that's hard. Let's talk about it."

Remember, one's light should never dim the other's.

Marriage Is Not the Opposite of Ambition

You can chase your dreams.
You can win awards, change cities, break ceilings.

But if you forget to hold hands on the way up,
You may find yourself standing alone at the top.

Chapter 25: In-Laws, Elders & Emotional Trespassing

In many cultures, especially in South Asia, marriage is not just between two people.
It's between two families. Two belief systems. Two generations of opinions, control, and emotional inheritance.

You don't just marry a person.
You marry their mother's expectations.
Their father's legacy.
Their sister's judgments.
And their family's definition of "how a spouse should behave."

While family can be a source of strength and support, in many modern marriages, it becomes a source of:

- Daily interference
- Manipulative advice
- Passive-aggressive guilt
- And a constant reminder: "You're never fully in control of your own relationship."

This chapter is about the boundary violations that look like affection, but feel like invasion.

The Everyday Interference

Not all family meddling is dramatic.

Most of it is subtle and relentlessly daily.

- The parent who calls every morning to "check in" but ends up giving unsolicited advice
- The mother-in-law who comments on how the food should be cooked
- The father-in-law who decides how the couple should spend money
- The constant suggestions on parenting, dressing, career, religion, rituals, and routines

And when one spouse (usually the one from that family) doesn't push back, the other feels:

- Ignored
- Powerless
- Outsider in their own home

It's not about hating your partner's family.
It's about not knowing where your relationship ends and theirs begins.

"He's Your Husband, Not Your Master"

"You're Her Husband, Not Her Servant"

This kind of toxic scripting often comes from parents, disguised as supportive words:

- "Don't be a doormat."

- "Why are you always adjusting?"
- "This is your house too."
- "She's too controlling."
- "He doesn't deserve your silence."

At first, it sounds like protection.
But often, it's planting doubt.

It shifts the focus from working through issues together to blaming the spouse behind their back.

What they never realise is:

Every time they take your side against your partner,
they're tearing apart the foundation of your marriage.

Loyalty Dilemma: Spouse or Parents?

This is one of the most painful battles in modern marriages:

"If you don't stand up for me… are you really with me?"

When one partner is repeatedly caught in the middle between the spouse and their parents, it becomes a no-win situation.

But when they don't take a stand, it sends a louder message:

"My parents come first.
You're replaceable."

This is especially common in:

- Joint families
- First-generation nuclear households
- Culturally traditional homes where "elders are never questioned"

But love cannot survive without boundaries.

The Myth of Harmless Involvement

"It's just advice."
"She means well."
"He's just concerned."
"That's how elders are."

This kind of rationalisation ignores one key fact:

Intentions don't matter if the outcome is emotional damage.

When your partner feels:

- Undermined
- Overruled
- Patronised
- Emotionally isolated
- Or turned into a punching bag for family frustrations

…it doesn't matter that your parents "didn't mean to hurt them."

The hurt is still real.

When Guilt Becomes a Weapon

Many families use guilt as control:

- "We gave you everything."
- "You've changed since marriage."
- "You don't call like you used to."
- "That person is taking you away from us."
- "Don't forget who stood by you first."

And you're left torn:

- Be a good son/daughter or a good partner?
- Keep the peace or protect your peace?
- Be loyal to your roots or loyal to your present?

But here's the hard truth:

If your marriage collapses, the same family who guilt-tripped you won't be the one living your life.

Boundaries Are Not Disrespect

Setting boundaries doesn't mean:

- Cutting off family
- Being rude

- Abandoning your roots
- Breaking culture

It means saying:

- "We'll make this decision together."
- "Let me speak to my spouse first."
- "Thanks for the advice, but we'll handle it."
- "Please don't talk about my partner that way."
- "We're figuring it out our way and we need space."

You can love your parents and still protect your marriage. That's not rebellion. That's maturity.

Tips to Create a Balanced Family Dynamic

- **Present a United Front:** Don't let family see cracks. Resolve issues privately.
- **Handle Your Own Family:** You speak to your parents. Let your partner speak to theirs.
- **Limit Oversharing:** Don't vent every fight to your family. It poisons their view of your spouse forever.
- **Choose Time Wisely:** Limit how often you allow "pop-ins," unsolicited calls, or surveillance-style check-ins.
- **Therapy (If Needed):** Family therapy or joint counselling can help when family overreach becomes too destructive.

Ask Yourselves

- "Do I defend you when my family crosses a line?"
- "Do you feel emotionally safe around my parents?"
- "Do I overshare private issues with them?"
- "Are our boundaries being enforced or being broken daily?"
- "Are we a team or two individuals pulled in opposite directions?"

Remember: You Are Building a New Family

Your marriage isn't a side project.
It's your primary emotional home.

If your parents or elders are constantly stepping inside that home without permission, it's your job to close the door, not slam it, but gently hold it.

Love your parents.
Respect your elders.
But don't sacrifice your peace just to preserve their pride.

Because no matter how close your family is…
it's the partner beside you every night who's carrying the real weight of your choices.

Chapter 26: The In-Law Equation – When Family Becomes a Third Wheel

They don't live with you.
They don't sleep in your bed.
But somehow, they're always in your marriage.

Whose family do we visit more?
Who gets to name the baby?
Why did she call again at 6 a.m.?
Why can't we make a decision without "consulting" them?

In-laws, well-meaning or not, often become a silent force in marital tension.

And it's not just mothers-in-law anymore.
It's siblings. Cousins. Grandparents. Parents on both sides.

Because today, the most common reason for stress isn't betrayal.
It's interference.

The Daily Phone Call That Feels Like Surveillance

One partner picks up their parent's call every day.
Shares everything. Gets "advice" regularly.

And the other starts to feel:

- Left out
- Judged
- Micromanaged
- Disrespected

It's subtle. But persistent.

Eventually, it becomes:

"Are we even a team? Or are you still their child first?"

The Guilt Trip

Phrases like:

- "We raised you better."
- "You've changed since marriage."
- "She controls you now."
- "He doesn't care about our side of the family."
- "Come home more often. We're growing old."

…aren't just comments.
They're emotional manipulation.

And if the spouse doesn't set boundaries,
The guilt silently bleeds into fights, decisions, and even intimacy.

The Power Struggle

Sometimes, parents try to:

- Control finances
- Dictate where the couple should live
- Decide on children's names, schools, even diets
- Insist on religious or cultural practices
- Expect regular updates, visits, and obedience

The partner feels helpless, torn between spouse and parent.

But here's the truth:

If you don't protect your partner from your family,
They'll eventually want protection from you.

What Silence Means

If your partner says:

- "Your mom is a little too involved."
- "I need space from your family."
- "I feel like I'm always being watched."

And you dismiss it with:

- "You're overthinking."
- "They mean well."
- "Just ignore them."
- "It's the same for everyone."

You're not being neutral.
You're taking a side, just not your partner's.

The Psychology of Loyalty

Many people think:

- "Being a good child means putting your parents first."
- "Marriage should never change my relationship with my parents."
- "If my spouse loves me, they should love my parents too."

But marriage is a shift in loyalty.

You don't abandon your parents.
But your first allegiance now is your spouse.

That's not disrespect.
That's emotional maturity.

When In-Laws Cross the Line

Some families:

- Badmouth the spouse
- Spy and report back
- Interfere in parenting
- Use money as leverage
- Compare constantly to exes or siblings

This isn't love.

This is sabotage dressed as concern.

Setting Boundaries Without Causing War

1. Speak as a couple.

"We've decided…" is more powerful than "I think…"

2. Don't complain about your spouse to your family.

They'll remember your anger, not your forgiveness.

3. Private issues stay private.

No fights should have an audience, especially not family.

4. Respect, but don't obey.

Parents deserve kindness. But not veto power over your marriage.

What to Say When They Overstep

- "We appreciate your care, but this is our decision."
- "We need some space to figure this out ourselves."
- "I know you love us. Please trust us to make the right choice."
- "Let's agree to disagree and move on."

And sometimes:

- "This is hurting our marriage. Please stop."

The Best In-Laws Know When to Step Back

They offer help, but don't force it.

They love the spouse like their own, but don't expect submission.

They give advice, but accept difference.

They show up, but don't stay too long.

They bless, but never burden.

Because the best gift parents can give their children is a chance to build their own home… on their own terms.

Chapter 27: Is Divorce the End or a New Beginning?

No one gets married planning to separate.
People walk into marriage with hope, commitment, and dreams.
So when it falls apart, it's not just the end of a relationship.
It feels like the death of a life imagined.

That's why divorce feels so devastating.
It's not just the loss of a partner.
It's the loss of:

- A version of yourself
- A shared future
- A set of roles and routines
- A family structure
- And sometimes, social identity

But here's the truth most people won't say aloud:

Divorce is not always a tragedy.
Sometimes, it's self-rescue.
Sometimes, it's survival.
And sometimes, it's the most loving thing you can do, for both of you.

The Stigma That Still Lingers

Even in modern society, divorced people carry invisible scars:

- "They couldn't adjust."
- "She must've been too independent."
- "He probably cheated."
- "They gave up too soon."
- "They must've married for the wrong reasons."

Rarely does anyone say:

- "They tried their best."
- "They outgrew each other."
- "They were brave to leave before bitterness consumed them."

We're conditioned to view staying as strength.
And leaving as failure.

But the reality is far more complex.

What Divorce Actually Means

Divorce doesn't mean:

- You're unlovable
- You're broken
- You're a bad parent
- You didn't try hard enough
- You're doomed to be alone

It simply means:

This partnership, in its current form, is no longer healthy or sustainable.

Sometimes, that's because of abuse or betrayal.
Other times, it's emotional starvation, mismatched values, life-altering change, or accumulated exhaustion.

Not all marriages die with a bang.
Some fade quietly, until one or both people realise that staying is no longer kind.

When Children Are Involved

Many couples stay "for the children."

But children don't just need a two-parent household.
They need:

- Emotional stability
- Safety
- Respect
- And a model of what love should look like

Growing up in a home where parents fight, avoid, criticise, or live in cold silence can teach children:

- That love is duty
- That suffering is normal
- That sacrifice means silence

Leaving doesn't make you a bad parent.
Staying in emotional chaos without repair might.

If you choose divorce, what matters most is how you do it:

- With dignity
- With minimal hostility
- With open communication and co-parenting commitment

Common Thoughts That Trap People

- "But what if I never find someone else?"
- "What will society think?"
- "I'm too old to start again."
- "Maybe I should just tolerate it."
- "I'll lose everything, money, time, security."

These thoughts are valid, but they are also fear-based.
They come from a place of survival, not growth.

Divorce is hard.
But so is living a lifetime unloved, unseen, or unheard.

The question isn't: Is divorce easy?
The question is: Is your marriage healthy enough to still nurture either of you?

Starting Over Isn't Failure, It's Rebirth

What happens after divorce?

- You grieve.
- You cry.
- You panic.
- You rebuild.
- You breathe.

Slowly, life returns.
Sometimes love does too, but this time, wiser.
And even if it doesn't, you return to yourself.

Because divorce doesn't just separate two people.
It often returns you to the person you used to be before you
started shrinking.

How to Exit With Grace

- Get legal clarity. Protect yourself without becoming
  aggressive.
- Keep dignity intact. Especially in public, around children,
  or on social media.
- Don't use children as leverage. Ever.
- Seek therapy. Divorce is both a logistical and emotional
  trauma.
- Create a support system. Friends, family, or even a support
  group.
- Give yourself time. You don't have to "move on" fast.
- Set boundaries. Especially if co-parenting continues.

Ask Yourself Honestly

- "Am I staying because I still believe in this marriage or just because I'm afraid?"
- "Have we both truly tried emotionally, honestly, and consistently?"
- "Do I still respect myself in this marriage?"
- "Would I want my child to live the kind of marriage I'm living now?"
- "If I met this person today, would I still choose them?"

You Are Allowed to Choose Peace

Whether you stay and heal, or leave and rebuild, your path is your own.

No one outside your relationship can understand its weight.
No book, society, family, or tradition can live your days for you.

And if you do choose to leave, it doesn't mean you failed.

It means you:

- Took accountability
- Refused to fake it
- Chose courage over comfort
- And began a new chapter

Because sometimes, the most powerful vow you can make…
Is to yourself.

Epilogue: What If It's Not Too Late?

Maybe you read this book to understand your own unraveling.
Or maybe you read it trying to prevent one.

Maybe you're still married.
Maybe you're divorced.
Maybe you're on the edge of either.

But if you take away one truth from these pages, let it be this:
You're not alone. And you're not crazy for feeling disappointed.

Because modern marriage was built on an outdated script.
It was handed down through generations with mismatched values,
clashing desires, and unrealistic promises.
We inherited fairytales and were handed reality, with no
guidebook in between.

This book wasn't meant to break hope.
It was meant to break silence.

There is no shame in leaving.
There is no shame in staying.

There is only shame in not asking the hard questions

- What are we doing this for?
- Who are we trying to please?
- And who are we hurting in the process?

Marriage doesn't fail because people are bad.
It fails because we enter it blindly, speak less, assume more, and wait too long.

But failure isn't always the end.
Sometimes it's the start of healing… as partners, co-parents, or individuals who finally saw the truth.

If you're willing to take responsibility, speak kindly, listen humbly, and love yourself without apology…

Then maybe, just maybe, your story doesn't have to end the way the world expects it to.

Because forever isn't a promise.
It's a choice you make again and again.
Not for others. Not for tradition.
But for a relationship that is worth rebuilding.

And if it's not?
Walk away with your head held high.

Not because you gave up.
But because you finally chose yourself.

Bonus Section: Reconnect or Reflect

Tools, Prompts & Exercises to Help You Go Deeper or Walk Away Wiser

Section 1: For Couples – Healing or Closure

1. The 10 Honest Questions Every Couple Must Ask

Sit down together. No phones. No defences. Just truth.

1. What is something I did recently that made you feel unseen or unloved?

2. What's one need of yours that you're scared to ask me for?

3. Do you feel more like my partner or my roommate these days? Why?

4. What would you change about our physical intimacy?

5. What's one thing you admire about me that you've never said aloud?

6. Have we stopped laughing together? If yes, when did it fade?

7. What do you miss about the early days of our relationship?

8. Do you feel you've grown or shrunk in this marriage?

9. Is there someone or something outside this marriage that you emotionally depend on?

10. What would a truly healed version of "us" look like?

2. The "Connection Currency" Game

Each partner writes down 5 things that make them feel most loved.
Example options:

- Undivided attention
- Physical affection
- Words of affirmation
- Acts of service
- Surprise gestures
- Deep conversation
- Shared goals or dreams
- Sexual touch or flirtation

Then, exchange lists.
For one week, focus only on the other person's list.
No judgment. No complaints. Just give.
Then, reflect together: Did anything shift?

3. The Marriage Autopsy Worksheet (For couples on the brink or post-breakup)

Use this to understand, not blame.

- When did we stop feeling like a team?
- What habits slowly killed our connection?
- Who tried harder and why didn't it work?
- What were the red flags we ignored?
- Did we stop communicating or just stop caring?
- What do I need to forgive myself for?
- What do I need to forgive you for?
- If I could go back in time, what would I do differently, not to change the outcome, but to protect my peace?

4. Rituals to Rebuild (If You Want To Try)

These are small, consistent acts, not grand gestures.

- **The 10-Minute Touch Base:** No phones, just sit and talk every evening. Even if it's awkward. Especially if it's awkward.
- **Weekly "We-Check":** Every Sunday, ask: "How was this week for you as my partner?"
- **Gratitude Ping-Pong:** One thank-you each per day. Not sarcastic. Not backhanded. Sincere.
- **Conflict Timeout Code:** Choose a word (e.g., "blueberry"). If either of you says it during a fight, pause. Resume after 10 mins.

Section 2: For Therapists and Counsellors

These prompts are for use in individual or joint sessions, to uncover buried beliefs and restore safety in communication.

Core Schema Exploration (Individual)

Ask each partner individually:

- What did you learn about love from your parents' relationship?
- When you feel ignored or disrespected, what belief about yourself gets triggered?
- What do you fear your partner really thinks about you?
- If your partner left tomorrow, what story would you tell yourself about why?

Conflict Cycle Mapping (Couples)

Draw this on a whiteboard or notebook:

- What triggers each person most?
- What's their automatic emotional reaction?
- What defence or behaviour follows?
- What core wound is activated beneath the surface?
- What's the unresolved need behind it?

Map this as a loop to visualise how both partners escalate or retreat.

The "Unsent Letter" Exercise

Each writes a letter to the other partner but doesn't send it. Read it out loud during session only if both agree.

- Begin with "If I could say anything without you interrupting…"
- End with "What I wish we could still be…"

Section 3: Sexual Intimacy Reset

Marriage often dies quietly between the sheets. This section helps couples rediscover, not just sex but safe, sacred intimacy.

1. The Yes-No-Maybe List

Each partner fills out a list of sexual and sensual activities as:

- Yes: I like this / open to try
- No: I'm not okay with this
- Maybe: I'm unsure but willing to explore

Compare lists. Talk without shame. Normalise differences.

2. Non-Sexual Touch Rituals

Schedule 20 minutes where:

- No clothes come off.
- No goals.
- Just touch: scalp massage, holding hands, lying face-to-face, or spooning.

Why? To rebuild safety and oxytocin, not just arousal.

3. Intimacy Dice (Verbal Edition)

Create two dice or draw two cards:

- One with locations (e.g., kitchen, balcony, car, under the stars)
- One with moods (e.g., playful, sensual, teasing, romantic, slow)

Pick a combo once a week. Keep it fun, consent-based, and lighthearted. Joy leads to desire.

4. "This Turns Me Off" Conversation

Each partner completes:

- "I feel sexually withdrawn when…"
- "I feel most desired when…"
- "One thing I wish you'd stop assuming is…"

No interruptions. No fixing. Just listen. Validate. Learn.

Acknowledgements

Because behind every brutally honest book is a very patient spouse.

First, to the countless couples whose stories, squabbles, and shared Wi-Fi passwords inspired this book, **thank you**. You made me realise that every marriage is weird, and that's exactly what makes it worth writing about.

To all the friends who said, "You should totally write about this," right after venting about their in-laws, mismatched libidos, or whose turn it was to unload the dishwasher, you were right. **I did.**

To the brave souls who let me ask them inappropriate questions over coffee in the name of "<u>research</u>", this book owes you more than caffeine.

To the readers: if you're flipping through these pages next to your partner while side-eyeing each other, **congrats**. That's called progress.

And finally, to my **wife**, who not only read this book but stayed married to me after reading it.
Thank you for not throwing it at me.
Thank you for helping me write about unhappy marriages while living in a happy (albeit occasionally loud) one.
You are proof that love can be honest, imperfect, and hilarious, and still work.

About the Author

Subin Mathews is a curious mind who believes that relationships are more complicated than quantum physics and far less predictable. A business owner by day and an observer of human behaviour by nature, Subin has spent years listening to people talk about their marriages… often in whispers, sighs, or silence.

He wrote Happy Wedding, Unhappy Marriage not as a therapist or expert, but as someone who has seen how quickly love can fade when no one speaks the truth. His goal isn't to fix marriages, it's to understand why they're breaking, and help people decide what's worth saving.

Subin lives in Mumbai with his wife, who's been more than a partner, she's been a co-navigator through every emotional storm. Together, they've built a relationship full of honesty, humour, and the occasional argument about who left the lights on.

When he's not writing or running his business, you'll find him exploring nature, testing ideas, or asking uncomfortable questions that somehow always lead to the heart of things.

www.ingramcontent.com/pod-product-compliance
Lightning Source LLC
Chambersburg PA
CBHW041314120726
48005CB00014B/1998